YOUR recipe could appear in our next cookbook!

Share your tried & true family favorites with us instantly at

www.gooseberrypatch.com

If you'd rather jot 'em down by hand, just mail this form to...

Gooseberry Patch • Cookbooks – Call for Recipes
2500 Farmers Dr., #110 • Columbus, OH 43235

If your recipe is selected for a book, you'll receive a FREE copy!

Please share only your original recipes or those that you have made your own over the years.

Recipe Name:

Number of Servings:

Any fond memories about this recipe? Special touches you like to add or handy shortcuts?

Ingredients (include specific measurements):

D1370761

Instructions (continue on back if needed):

Special Code: **cookbookspage**

Over ➤

Extra space for recipe if needed:

Tell us about yourself...

Your complete contact information is needed so that we can send you your FREE cookbook, if your recipe is published. Phone numbers and email addresses are kept private and will only be used if we have questions about your recipe.

Name:

Address:

City: State: Zip:

Email:

Daytime Phone:

Thank you! Vickie & Jo Ann

Mom's
VERY BEST Recipes

pumpkin loaf
2 c. flour
1 1/2 c. brown sugar
3 eggs

Gooseberry Patch
2500 Farmers Dr., #110
Columbus, OH 43235

www.gooseberrypatch.com

1·800·854·6673

Do you have a tried & true recipe...

tip, craft or memory that you'd like to see featured in a **Gooseberry
Patch** cookbook? Visit our website at **www.gooseberrypatch.com**
to share them with us instantly. If you'd rather jot them down by hand,
use the handy form in the front of this book and send them to...

Gooseberry Patch
Attn: Cookbook Dept.
2500 Farmers Dr., #110
Columbus, OH 43235

Don't forget to include the number of servings your recipe makes,
plus your name, address, phone number and email address.
If we select your recipe, your name will appear right along
with it...and you'll receive a **FREE** copy of the cookbook!

Contents

Dedication

For mothers everywhere who know how to warm heart & soul with a kind smile, a big hug and a bowl of homemade chicken soup.

Appreciation

To all of you who gave us cherished recipes and memories of Mom, Grandma and your own families, thanks!

Breakfast & Brunch

Recipes

Mom's Cheesy Hashbrowns

Valerie Hendrickson
Cedar Springs, MI

*My mother used to make this scrumptious dish the old-fashioned way,
starting with hand-shredded boiled potatoes. This version is
simplified, yet is still full of hearty homestyle flavor!*

1/4 c. butter
1 sweet onion, chopped
2 c. shredded Cheddar cheese
1 c. sour cream

30-oz. pkg. country-style frozen
    shredded hashbrowns,
    thawed

Melt butter in a medium saucepan over medium heat. Add onion and
cook until translucent, about 5 minutes. Mix in cheese and continue
stirring until melted. Remove from heat; stir in sour cream. Gently fold
mixture into hashbrowns. Spoon into a greased 2-quart casserole
dish. Bake, uncovered, at 350 degrees for 60 to 75 minutes, until
heated through and top is golden. Serves 6 to 8.

Add a dash of color to the breakfast table...it wakes everyone up!
Mix & match cheery plates, set out spunky retro juice glasses
and arrange a bunch of daisies in a jelly-jar vase.

Sausage & Potato Bake

Lori Comer
Kernersville, NC

One snowy weekend I wanted to fix something special for my family,
so I tried this recipe and it is a real keeper! Just add sourdough toast
and a fresh fruit salad for a hearty breakfast.

1 lb. mild ground pork sausage
1 lb. hot ground pork sausage
10-3/4 oz. can cream of
    chicken soup
8-oz. container French
    onion dip

8-oz. container sour cream
2 c. shredded sharp Cheddar
    cheese
30-oz. pkg. frozen shredded
    hashbrowns with peppers
    and onion, thawed

Brown sausage in a skillet over medium heat; drain and set aside.
In a large bowl, combine remaining ingredients except hashbrowns;
stir until well blended. Fold in hashbrowns and sausage; transfer to a
greased 13"x9" baking pan. Bake, uncovered, at 350 degrees for 45 to
55 minutes, until bubbly and golden. Makes 10 to 12 servings.

Make-ahead breakfast casseroles are super time-savers
for busy mornings. Assemble the night before, cover and refrigerate,
then just pop in the oven...breakfast is served!

Old-Fashioned Doughnuts

Cathy Johnson
Oregon, WI

*My mom was a wonderful cook, and her scrumptious homemade
doughnuts were a family favorite.*

1 c. milk
1 T. vinegar
1 c. cold mashed potatoes
4 c. all-purpose flour
1 c. sugar
3 eggs, beaten
1 T. butter, softened

4 t. baking powder
1 t. salt
1 t. nutmeg
1/2 t. mace
1 t. vanilla extract
peanut oil for deep frying
Garnish: sugar

In a small bowl, mix together milk and vinegar; let stand for a few
minutes. In a large bowl, mix together remaining ingredients except
frying oil and garnish. Add milk mixture and stir well. Turn out 1/3 of
dough onto a floured surface. Roll out dough 1/2-inch thick. Cut with
a doughnut cutter. In a deep fryer over high heat, heat several inches
of oil to 375 degrees. Add doughnuts, a few at a time. Doughnuts will
sink when put into the hot oil. When they rise to the top, turn and
watch until golden. When golden on both sides, remove with a slotted
spoon. Drain on a brown paper bag or paper towels. Roll warm
doughnuts in sugar. Makes 3 dozen.

Doughnut kabobs...a fun idea
for a brunch buffet! Slide
bite-size doughnuts onto
wooden skewers and stand
the skewers in a tall vase
for easy serving.

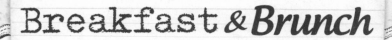
French Breakfast Puffs

Lisa Stanish
Houston, TX

These are my mother's mini muffins...they're a wonderful treat with a cup of hot tea.

2/3 c. butter, divided	1-1/2 t. baking powder
1/2 c. sugar	1/4 t. nutmeg
1 egg, beaten	1/2 t. salt
1-1/2 c. all-purpose flour	1/2 c. milk

In a large bowl, blend 1/3 cup butter and sugar. Add egg and mix until fluffy. In a separate bowl, stir together flour, baking powder, nutmeg and salt. Gradually add flour mixture to butter mixture, alternating with milk. Fill greased mini muffin cups 2/3 full. Bake at 350 degrees for 15 minutes, or until golden. Remove from muffin cups and roll first in remaining butter, melted, then in Cinnamon-Sugar. Makes 4 dozen.

Cinnamon-Sugar:

1/2 c. sugar	2 T. cinnamon

In a small bowl, mix ingredients together.

Surprise Mom with breakfast in bed...and it doesn't have to be just on Mothers' Day! Fill a tray with breakfast goodies, the morning paper and a bright blossom tucked into an egg cup.

Cream Cheese Crescent Rolls

Kris Thompson
Ripley, NY

My mother received this recipe from my cousin many years ago.
It's quick & easy...no one can eat just one!

3-oz. pkg. cream cheese,
   softened
1/4 c. sugar

1 T. lemon juice
8-oz. tube refrigerated crescent
   rolls

In a small bowl, blend cream cheese, sugar and lemon juice until smooth. Separate rolls; spread each roll with cream cheese mixture. Roll up, starting at one long edge. Arrange rolls on a lightly greased baking sheet. Bake at 375 degrees for 12 to 15 minutes, until golden. Makes 8 rolls.

Buttery Lemon Curd

Sandy Roy
Crestwood, KY

An old recipe from England. This lemony spread is irresistible on scones,
toast and muffins, even on slices of pound cake!

1 c. butter
2 c. sugar
3 eggs, beaten

1/2 c. lemon juice
1 T. lemon zest

In a double boiler over simmering water, melt butter. Stir in remaining ingredients. Cook, stirring occasionally, for one hour, or until sauce thickens and reaches 160 degrees on a candy thermometer. Transfer to a covered container; keep refrigerated. Makes 3 cups.

Tuck a jar of Buttery Lemon Curd into a gift basket of extra-special scones. Stir up a favorite scone recipe or mix, pat out the dough and cut out with a heart-shaped cookie cutter...sweet!

Cinnamon Knots

Connie Spivey
Blue Springs, MO

My mom used to make these breakfast treats when I was small. I can remember helping to dip them and then tie the knots. They smell wonderful baking and taste even better!

1 env. active dry yeast	1 egg, beaten
3/4 c. warm water, divided	1/2 t. salt
1/2 c. shortening	3 c. all-purpose flour
1 c. plus 3 T. sugar, divided	1 c. butter, melted
1/2 c. milk	3 T. cinnamon

Dissolve yeast in 1/4 cup very warm water, 110 to 115 degrees; set aside. In a saucepan over medium heat, combine remaining water, shortening and 3 tablespoons sugar. Stir until sugar dissolves. Remove from heat; add milk and cool slightly. Pour mixture into a large bowl; add egg, salt and yeast mixture. Add flour and mix well. Cover and let rise in a warm place until double in size, about one hour. Roll out dough on a floured surface to 1/2-inch thick. Cut dough into 6-inch by 1/2-inch strips. Place melted butter in a small bowl. Mix remaining sugar and cinnamon together in a separate bowl. Dip each strip into butter and then into sugar mixture. Tie each strip into a knot; place on greased baking sheets. Cover and let rise until double in size, about one hour. Bake at 350 degrees for about 12 minutes, until golden. Makes 2-1/2 to 3 dozen.

Invite a best girlfriend over to share tea and muffins on a Saturday morning...it's a terrific way for the two of you to spend time catching up!

Butter Rum Muffins

Diana Krol
Nickerson, KS

My grandson, Kanon, loves this breakfast treat...I think you will too!

2/3 c. butter, softened
1-1/3 c. sugar
4 eggs, beaten
2 T. baking powder
1/4 t. salt

1 t. butter flavoring
1 t. rum extract
2 c. milk
4 c. all-purpose flour
12-oz. pkg. butterscotch chips

In a large bowl, blend together butter, sugar and eggs. Mix in baking powder, salt and flavorings. Alternately mix in milk and flour; fold in chips. Divide evenly into greased muffin cups, filling 2/3 full. Bake at 350 degrees for 15 to 20 minutes, until a toothpick tests done. Makes 3 dozen.

God could not be everywhere, and therefore
he made mothers.
-Rudyard Kipling

Blueberry-Rhubarb Muffins

*Paula Marchesi
Lenhartsville, PA*

On summer Sunday mornings, my brother and I could smell these delicious muffins baking before we went to church. We'd hurry to get dressed so we could enjoy them before we left. Mom always made a double batch...we were never satisfied with just one! Every time I bite into one of these yummy muffins, I'm taken back to those carefree summer days.

1/4 c. butter, softened
3/4 c. sugar
1 egg, beaten
1/4 c. sour cream
1-1/2 c. all-purpose flour
2 t. baking powder
1 t. salt

1/3 c. milk
1 c. blueberries
1 c. rhubarb, chopped
cinnamon-sugar to taste
Optional: butter or cream
    cheese, softened

In a small bowl, blend butter and sugar. Add egg and sour cream; mix well. Combine flour, baking powder and salt in a separate bowl; add to butter mixture, alternating with milk. Fold in berries and rhubarb. Fill 12 greased or paper-lined muffin cups about 2/3 full. Sprinkle with cinnamon-sugar. Bake at 400 degrees for 20 to 25 minutes, until a toothpick tests clean. Cool in tin for 5 minutes before removing muffins to a wire rack. Spread with butter or cream cheese, if desired. Makes one dozen.

Mmm...fresh-baked muffins! Most muffin batters can be stirred up the night before and can even be scooped into muffin cups. Simply cover and refrigerate...in the morning, pop them in the oven.

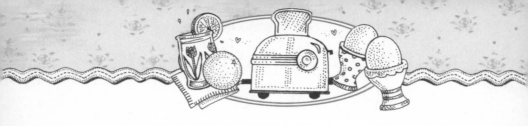

Mom's Sweet Apple Omelet

Kristy Markners
Fort Mill, SC

This is a recipe my mom has been making as long as I can remember. My brother and I used to fight over who could eat the last serving...it's that good!

4 c. applesauce
3 eggs, beaten
1 c. sugar

1 T. cinnamon
Optional: 1 to 1-1/2 T. flour

Whisk together all ingredients, adding flour if applesauce is very runny. Pour into an ungreased 9" pie plate. Bake, uncovered, at 350 degrees for one hour, or until center is firm. Scoop and serve warm. Makes 8 servings.

A hearty homestyle breakfast that's welcome on the chilliest morning! Cook up frozen diced potatoes in a cast-iron skillet, then use the back of a spoon to make 6 wells. Break an egg into each and bake at 350 degrees for 12 to 14 minutes, until eggs are set. Serve piping hot, right from the skillet.

Baked Garden Omelet

Gwen Hudson
Madison Heights, VA

I serve this scrumptious vegetable-packed dish year 'round for brunch or a light lunch. Feel free to add your favorite fresh veggies!

1 c. shredded Pepper Jack
  cheese
1-1/2 c. broccoli, chopped
2 tomatoes, coarsely chopped
2 c. shredded Cheddar cheese

1 c. milk
1/4 c. all-purpose flour
1/2 t. salt
3 eggs, beaten

In an ungreased 8"x8" baking pan, layer Pepper Jack cheese, broccoli, tomatoes and Cheddar cheese; set aside. In a bowl, beat milk, flour, salt and eggs until smooth. Pour over cheese mixture. Bake, uncovered, at 350 degrees for 40 to 45 minutes, until set. Let stand 10 minutes before cutting into squares. Serves 6 to 8.

Keep tea towels at your fingertips on the counter by the kitchen sink.
Slip rolled-up towels into a vintage milk bottle carrier.

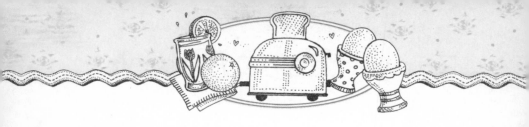

Spiced Zucchini Bars

Erin Carnes
Gaines, MI

This is one of many recipes I got from my mother-in-law. These yummy bars are one of the first things I make when the zucchini is ready to pick in my garden. I love to eat them for breakfast! Double the frosting recipe if you like it extra-thick.

2 c. all-purpose flour
2 t. baking soda
1/2 t. salt
2 t. cinnamon
3 eggs, beaten
1 c. oil

2 c. sugar
1 t. vanilla extract
1 t. lemon juice
1 c. raisins
2 c. zucchini, grated
3/4 c. chopped nuts

Combine dry ingredients in a small bowl; set aside. In a separate bowl, whisk together eggs, oil, sugar, vanilla and lemon juice. Gradually add flour mixture to egg mixture. Fold in remaining ingredients; pour into a greased and floured 15"x10" jelly-roll pan. Bake at 325 degrees for 25 to 35 minutes, until lightly golden. Cool; frost with Cream Cheese Frosting. Cut into bars. Makes 3 dozen.

Cream Cheese Frosting:

1/2 c. butter, softened
8-oz. pkg. cream cheese, softened

1 t. vanilla extract
1 c. powdered sugar

Beat all ingredients until smooth.

Dress up these easy, pleasing bars for a brunch buffet! Instead of cutting them into bars or squares, cut diagonally across the pan for pretty little diamonds.

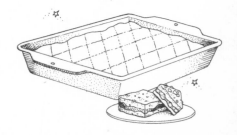

Butterscotch-Pecan Pull-Aparts

Marissa Pinon
Fairborn, OH

My mom used to bake these before I left for school...I was happy
to get up early just to enjoy them!

18-count pkg. frozen rolls
3.4-oz. pkg. cook & serve
   butterscotch pudding mix

1/2 c. brown sugar, packed
1/2 c. chopped pecans
1/2 c. butter, melted

Spray a Bundt® pan with non-stick vegetable spray; line with frozen
rolls. Mix together dry pudding mix, brown sugar and pecans. Pour
mixture over rolls; drizzle with melted butter. Cover with plastic wrap;
let rise for 12 hours. Uncover; bake at 350 degrees for 25 minutes,
until golden. Cool before serving. Serves 6.

Coming-Home Coffee Cake

Stephanie Ambler
Zanesville, IN

My mother's recipe...this coffee cake was one of my brother's
first requests after returning home from Iraq.

1 c. brown sugar, packed
2 t. cinnamon
1/2 t. nutmeg
18-1/2 oz. pkg. yellow cake mix
3.4-oz. pkg. instant vanilla
   pudding mix

3.4-oz. pkg. instant butterscotch
   pudding mix
4 eggs, beaten
3/4 c. oil or applesauce
1 c. water

Mix brown sugar and spices; set aside. Mix together remaining
ingredients; pour into an ungreased 13"x9" baking pan. Sprinkle with
brown sugar mixture; cut through with a knife to create swirls. Bake
at 350 degrees for 20 minutes. Reduce heat to 325 degrees; bake
an additional 40 to 50 minutes, until a toothpick tests clean. Makes
12 servings.

Herbed Sausage Quiche

Cherylann Smith
Efland, NC

My kids love this tasty quiche...they ask for it at least once a week! It's a super make-ahead too...make several quiches at a time, bake them for the first 15 minutes and freeze. To serve, thaw in the fridge and bake at 350 degrees for 20 to 30 minutes, until heated through.

1 c. ground pork sausage,
   browned and drained
3 eggs, beaten
1 c. whipping cream
salt and pepper to taste
1 sprig fresh rosemary, chopped

1 t. Italian seasoning
1 t. dried basil
1 t. dried thyme
1 t. dried oregano
1 c. shredded Cheddar cheese
9-inch deep-dish pie crust

In a large bowl, mix together all ingredients except pie crust; spread into crust. Bake, uncovered, at 450 degrees for 15 minutes. Reduce heat to 350 degrees and bake an additional 15 minutes. Cut into wedges to serve. Makes 8 servings.

Add a savory, quick & easy crumb crust to your favorite quiche. Spread
2-1/2 tablespoons softened butter in a pie plate, then
firmly press 2-1/2 cups buttery cracker crumbs or seasoned
dry bread crumbs into the butter. Freeze until firm, pour in
filling and bake as directed.

Summer Swiss Quiche

Rebecca Barna
Blairsville, PA

This is an excellent breakfast & brunch dish to serve when gardens
kick in. My family really enjoys it...I bet yours will too!

1/2 lb. bacon
2 zucchini, thinly sliced
1 green pepper, chopped
1 onion, chopped
1 to 2 T. butter or olive oil

8 eggs, beaten
1 c. milk
1/4 c. biscuit baking mix
5 slices Swiss cheese

In a skillet over medium heat, cook bacon until crisp; drain and set
aside. In a separate skillet over medium heat, sauté zucchini, green
pepper and onion in butter or oil. In a bowl, mix eggs, milk and
baking mix together. Pour egg mixture into a greased 13"x9" baking
pan. Spoon zucchini mixture over egg mixture. Cover with crumbled
bacon; arrange cheese slices on top. Bake, uncovered, at 350 degrees
for 30 to 35 minutes, until a toothpick inserted near the center comes
out clean. Cut into squares. Makes 8 to 10 servings.

Bake a quiche in muffin or custard cups for oh-so simple individual
servings. When making minis, reduce the baking time by about
10 minutes and check for doneness with a toothpick.

Yummy Brunch Strata

Lynn Williams
Muncie, IN

My grandma was famous for this feed-a-crowd dish at the weekly brunch her church used to hold after Sunday services. Just add a tray of sweet rolls, a big pot of hot coffee and fellowship!

1/3 c. oil
2 c. cooked ham, diced
3 c. sliced mushrooms
3 c. zucchini, diced
1-1/2 c. onion, diced
1-1/2 c. green, red or yellow
   pepper, diced
2 cloves garlic, minced

2 8-oz. pkgs. cream cheese,
   softened
1/2 c. half-and-half
1 doz. eggs, beaten
4 c. day-old bread, cubed
3 c. shredded Cheddar cheese
salt and pepper to taste

Heat oil in a large skillet over medium-high heat. Add ham and vegetables; sauté for 3 to 5 minutes, until tender. Drain; set aside. In a large bowl, beat together cream cheese and half-and-half until smooth. Stir in vegetable mixture and remaining ingredients; blend lightly. Pour into 2 greased 11"x7" baking pans. Bake, uncovered, at 350 degrees for 35 to 40 minutes, until a knife inserted near the center comes out clean. Let stand 10 minutes; cut into squares. Makes 16 servings.

Start a kitchen journal to note favorite recipes and family members' preferences. It'll make meal planning a snap!

Rise & Shine Sandwiches

Dale Duncan
Waterloo, IA

Sure, you could get these from your local drive-through, but why?
They're easy to make and easy to adapt to your own tastes!

2-1/4 c. buttermilk biscuit
   baking mix
1/2 c. water
8 pork sausage breakfast patties

8 eggs, beaten
1 T. butter
salt and pepper to taste
8 slices American cheese

In a bowl, combine biscuit mix with water until just blended. Turn onto a floured surface and knead for one minute. Roll out to 1/2-inch thickness. Cut out 8 biscuits with a 3-inch round biscuit cutter. Arrange on an ungreased baking sheet. Bake at 425 degrees for 8 to 10 minutes, until golden. Meanwhile, in a skillet over medium heat, brown sausage patties; drain. In a separate skillet over low heat, scramble eggs in butter to desired doneness; season with salt and pepper. Split biscuits; top each biscuit bottom with a sausage patty, a spoonful of eggs and a cheese slice. Add biscuit tops and serve immediately. Makes 8 servings.

If you're making biscuits
and there's no biscuit cutter handy,
just try Mom's little
trick...use a glass tumbler
to cut out the dough.

Whole-Wheat Cinnamon Scones

Amy Wentzel
Lancaster, PA

I came up with this recipe as a yummy way to sneak some whole-grain goodness into my family's breakfast. My four young children and I love to make them together!

2-1/4 c. whole-wheat flour
2 T. sugar
1 T. plus 1 t. baking powder
1/2 t. salt
2 t. cinnamon
1/4 c. chilled butter

1/2 c. cinnamon baking chips
3/4 c. milk
1/4 c. ricotta cheese
1 T. honey
2 t. vanilla extract

In a large bowl, combine flour, sugar, baking powder, salt and cinnamon. With a pastry blender, cut butter into flour mixture. Add cinnamon chips; mix with a fork. In a separate bowl, combine remaining ingredients. Make a well in flour mixture; add milk mixture all at once. Stir with a fork just until a soft dough forms. Lightly knead the dough in the bowl until dough holds together; form into a ball. Transfer dough to a parchment paper-lined baking sheet. Form dough into an 8-inch round. Score lightly into 8 wedges, but do not separate the wedges. Bake at 400 degrees for 18 to 23 minutes, until golden. Serves 8.

Whip up a crock of maple butter to serve with freshly baked scones. Just combine 1/2 cup softened butter with 3/4 cup maple syrup and beat until fluffy...yum!

Multi-Grain Waffles

Kay Marone
Des Moines, IA

Get everyone's day off to a healthy start with
these toasty, nutty-tasting waffles!

1/2 c. long-cooking oats,
   uncooked
2 c. buttermilk
2/3 c. whole-wheat flour
2/3 c. all-purpose flour
1/4 c. toasted wheat germ
1-1/2 t. baking powder
1/2 t. baking soda

1/4 t. salt
1 t. cinnamon
2 eggs, beaten
1/4 c. brown sugar, packed
1 T. oil
2 t. vanilla extract
Garnish: butter, maple syrup

Mix oats and buttermilk in a large bowl; let stand for 15 minutes. In a separate bowl, whisk together flours, wheat germ, baking powder, baking soda, salt and cinnamon. Add eggs, brown sugar, oil and vanilla to oat mixture; mix well. Add oat mixture to flour mixture; stir just until moistened. Add batter by 2/3 cupfuls to a preheated, greased waffle iron. Bake according to manufacturer's instructions until crisp and golden, about 4 to 5 minutes. Garnish as desired. Makes 8.

Homemade waffles on a weekday morning...what a treat!
Waffles can be stored in plastic freezer bags for up to
a month. To serve, place waffles in a single layer on a
baking sheet, cover with aluminum foil and bake at
350 degrees for about 10 minutes, until toasty.

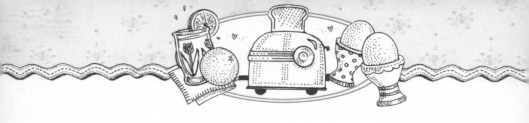

Egg Casserole Deluxe

Natasha Morris
Ulysses, KS

My youngest daughter made this for her sister's bridal shower...it was a big hit with the bride-to-be and the guests! For a crowd, simply double the recipe and bake in a 13"x9" baking pan.

1 to 2 T. butter
1 doz. eggs, beaten
8-oz. container sour cream
4-oz. jar sliced mushrooms,
   drained

1/2 c. shredded Cheddar cheese
2.8-oz. pkg. pre-cooked bacon,
   crumbled and divided

Melt butter in a large skillet over medium heat. Add eggs; cook and stir until softly scrambled. Stir in sour cream, mushrooms, cheese and half of bacon. Transfer to a lightly greased 8"x8" baking pan. Sprinkle remaining bacon on top. Bake, uncovered, at 350 degrees for 30 minutes. Serves 8.

Light and fizzy...the perfect drink for brunch. Combine 6 cups chilled pineapple juice, one cup sugar and one cup lime juice. Stir in 2 liters sparkling water and serve over crushed ice, garnished with skewers of fruit.

Farmer's Hearty Breakfast

Sandy Churchill
West Bridgewater, MA

On a chilly fall or winter day, this is one of my family's most-requested comfort-food meals. It's also a terrific way to sneak some broccoli onto their plates!

6 to 8 frozen hashbrown patties
16-oz. pkg. frozen chopped
 broccoli, thawed
1 lb. cooked ham, cubed
6 eggs, beaten
8-oz. container sour cream
1/4 c. milk
1 t. garlic salt
1 t. dried, minced onion
8-oz. pkg. shredded Cheddar
 cheese

Arrange hashbrown patties in the bottom of an ungreased 11"x9" baking pan. Arrange broccoli in a single layer; layer ham over broccoli. In a large bowl, stir together remaining ingredients except cheese; pour over ham. Top with cheese. Bake, uncovered, at 350 degrees for 40 minutes, or until heated through and cheese is melted. Serves 6 to 8.

For delicious, moist scrambled eggs, whisk a teaspoon each of mayonnaise and water into two eggs. Cook over low heat in a teaspoon of butter, until set to desired firmness.

Honey-Baked Bananas

Amy Greenlee
Carterville, IL

My mom shared this recipe for luscious honeyed bananas.

6 bananas, halved lengthwise
2 T. butter, melted

1/4 c. honey
2 T. lemon juice

Arrange bananas in an ungreased 13"x9" baking pan. Blend remaining ingredients; brush over bananas. Bake, uncovered, at 350 degrees for about 15 minutes, turning occasionally. Serves 6.

Breakfast Banana "Soup"

Lisa Vance
Lowellville, OH

My kids love this, and it's very easy to make. Enjoy it spooned over hot oatmeal or cold cereal, or just eat it right out of the bowl.

2 c. whipping cream
1/4 c. brown sugar, packed
1/2 t. cinnamon

1/2 t. vanilla extract
5 bananas, sliced into bite-size
   pieces

In a bowl, mix together cream, brown sugar, cinnamon and vanilla until blended. Stir in bananas. Cover and refrigerate overnight. Serves 4 to 6.

Bananas will ripen quickly if placed overnight in
a brown paper grocery bag.

Breakfast & *Brunch*

Mom's Yummy Fruit Bowl

Dallas Bieker
Manhattan, KS

My mom makes this year 'round, but it is especially refreshing in winter when fresh fruit isn't abundant. My children think it's a terrific way to eat fruit, because it tastes like dessert!

16-oz. pkg. frozen strawberries, partially thawed
15-oz. can mandarin oranges, drained
20-oz. can pineapple tidbits, drained and juice reserved

3.4-oz. pkg. instant French vanilla pudding mix
2 bananas, sliced

Combine strawberries, oranges and pineapple in a large bowl. In a small bowl, stir together dry pudding mix and reserved juice until smooth. Add to fruit mixture; gently stir to coat. Cover and refrigerate 2 to 3 hours. Stir to blend; fold in bananas. Serves 6.

Grammy's Creamy Fruit Salad

Jennifer Tolbert
Loganville, GA

Five generations of our family have enjoyed this recipe!

2 eggs, beaten
5 T. lemon juice
10-1/2 oz. pkg. mini marshmallows

16-oz. can pineapple chunks, drained
2 c. seedless grapes, halved
2 c. whipping cream

In a double boiler over medium heat, combine eggs and lemon juice. Whisk constantly until mixture thickens to a pudding-like consistency, 8 to 10 minutes. Place marshmallows in a large bowl. Pour egg mixture over marshmallows; stir to combine. Add pineapple and grapes; stir. In a separate bowl, whip cream until thickened and soft peaks form. Fold cream into fruit mixture. Cover; refrigerate overnight before serving. Serves 10 to 12.

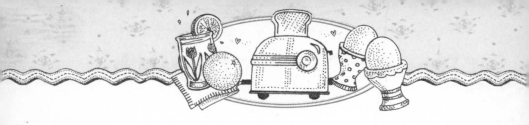

Chuckwagon Breakfast Skillet

JoAnn

For a head start on this hearty, delicious breakfast, the potatoes can be cooked ahead of time.

2 lbs. potatoes, peeled and
   cubed
1/2 lb. bacon, chopped
1 to 2 T. oil
1 green or red pepper, sliced
1 onion, sliced
2 c. sliced mushrooms

salt and pepper to taste
2 c. shredded Colby cheese
2 T. butter
8 eggs
Optional: fresh chives or parsley,
   chopped

Add potatoes to a saucepan of boiling water. Cook over medium heat for 12 to 15 minutes, until tender; drain. Meanwhile, in a large skillet over medium heat, cook bacon until crisp. Remove bacon to a paper towel; reserve some of drippings in skillet. Add potatoes and one to 2 tablespoons oil to skillet; sauté until golden. Add peppers, onion, mushrooms, salt and pepper; sauté until vegetables are tender. Drain; stir in bacon. Top with cheese; reduce heat to low. In a separate skillet over medium heat, scramble or fry eggs in butter as desired. To serve, spoon potato mixture into a large serving dish; top with eggs. Garnish, if desired. Serves 6 to 8.

Keep shopping simple...have a shopping
list that includes all ingredients you
normally use, plus a few blank lines
for special items. You'll breeze
right down the aisles!

Ham & Gruyère Egg Cups

Sonya Labbe
Santa Monica, CA

This recipe is always on our Sunday brunch table. It is easy,
simple and tasty...it's very pretty too!

12 thin slices deli ham
3/4 c. shredded Gruyère cheese
1 doz. eggs

salt and pepper to taste
1 c. half-and-half
2 T. grated Parmesan cheese

Spray a muffin tin with non-stick vegetable spray. Line each muffin
cup with a slice of ham folded in half. Top each ham slice with one
tablespoon Gruyère cheese, an egg cracked into the cup, a sprinkle of
salt and pepper, one tablespoon half-and-half and 1/2 teaspoon
Parmesan cheese. Place muffin tin on a baking sheet. Bake at
450 degrees for 15 minutes, until eggs are set. Allow baked eggs to
cool for several minutes before removing them from the muffin tin.
Makes one dozen.

Liven up plain orange juice with a splash of ginger ale or
sparkling white grape juice...serve in stemmed glasses
for a festive breakfast beverage.

Uncle Dave's Oven Pancakes

Anne Ptacnik
Yuma, CO

My late Uncle Dave often made these yummy pancakes for breakfast when I was a guest at his home. Now, whenever I prepare them, I think about him and how he always made everything special.

1/4 c. butter
4 eggs, beaten
2 c. milk

1 c. all-purpose flour
1/2 c. sugar
Garnish: butter, pancake syrup

Place butter in a 13"x9" baking pan; melt in a 400-degree oven. Add eggs, milk, flour and sugar to a bowl; whisk until thoroughly combined. Pour mixture over melted butter. Bake at 350 degrees for 30 minutes. Serve with butter and syrup. Serves 4 to 6.

Homemade Pancake Syrup

Denise Louk
Garnett, KS

This is the only syrup used at our house! My aunt gave me this recipe fifteen years ago, shortly after I was married. Make it as thick or thin as you like, just adjust the amount of water used.

1 c. sugar
1 c. corn syrup

1/2 c. hot water
1/2 t. maple flavoring

Combine sugar, corn syrup and hot water in a saucepan over medium-high heat. Bring to a boil, stirring constantly. Add maple flavoring. Simmer for 5 to 10 minutes. Serve warm. Makes 2 cups.

Scottish Pancakes

Chris Hutcheson
Sheffield, England

My husband is Scottish and has fond memories of eating his mum's pancakes. It's only recently that I dared to try making them, for fear of utter failure when compared with Mum's! After adding my own improvements, our five-year-old son now insists on them on Saturday mornings, with butter, just the same as his dad. I love them too, especially with the luscious blueberry topping. Yum!

2/3 c. self-rising flour
1/2 T. baking powder
3-1/2 T. sugar
1 t. vanilla extract

1 egg
7/8 c. milk
1 to 2 T. butter
Garnish: Greek-style yogurt

Sift flour and baking powder into a bowl; add sugar and vanilla. Create a well; add egg to well and whisk together ingredients. Add milk gradually; mix until smooth. In a skillet over medium heat, melt butter. When butter starts to bubble, add 2/3 cup batter to skillet per pancake, forming 2-inch pancakes. When bubbles start to appear on surface of pancakes, flip them over; cook one to 2 minutes on each side. Serve topped with yogurt and Blueberry Syrup. Serves 2.

Blueberry Syrup:

1 c. blueberries

1/2 c. maple syrup

Place berries and syrup in a small saucepan over medium-low heat. Simmer for 2 to 3 minutes, until warmed through.

Keep a tin of apple pie spice on hand to jazz up pancakes, muffins and coffee cakes...a quick shake adds cinnamon, nutmeg and allspice all at once.

Peanut Butter & Jelly French Toast

Julie Perkins
Anderson, IN

Who can resist the classic taste of peanut butter & jelly?

4 slices white bread
1/2 c. creamy peanut butter
2 T. grape jelly
3 eggs, beaten

1/4 c. milk
2 T. butter
Garnish: powdered sugar

Use bread, peanut butter and jelly to make 2 sandwiches; set aside. In a bowl, whisk together eggs and milk. Dip each sandwich into egg mixture. Melt butter in a non-stick skillet over medium heat. Add sandwiches to skillet and cook until golden, about 2 to 3 minutes on each side. Sprinkle with powdered sugar; cut diagonally into triangles. Serves 2.

Looking for a new message board? Hang an old-fashioned washboard for a whimsical way to keep notes organized! Use buttons hot-glued to magnets to hold messages and photos in place.

Dad's Famous French Toast

Annette Mullan
North Arlington, NJ

When I was growing up, my dad fixed French toast every Sunday morning from his own recipe. Dad is no longer with us, but recently our family got together for a weekend and we made his French toast for everyone! It's still the best I've ever had.

4 eggs, beaten
1/2 c. milk
1/3 c. sugar
1 t. vanilla extract
1/8 t. cinnamon
1 loaf sliced white bread
Garnish: butter, pancake syrup,
powdered sugar

Mix eggs, milk, sugar, vanilla and cinnamon in a large bowl. Dip bread into mixture, one slice at a time. Spray an electric or regular griddle with non-stick vegetable spray. Add bread slices; cook over medium heat until golden on both sides. Serve with desired garnishes. Serves 8.

For a touch of whimsy at the breakfast table, use an old-fashioned cow-shaped creamer to hold milk for cereal, oatmeal and hot coffee.

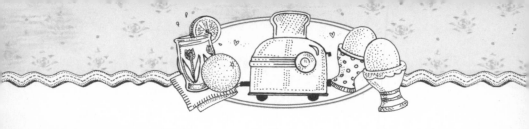

Mile-High Biscuits

Sharon Dennison
Floyds Knobs, IN

These biscuits are light, fluffy and oh-so good!

3 c. all-purpose flour
2 T. sugar
4-1/2 t. baking powder
3/4 t. cream of tartar

3/4 t. salt
3/4 c. shortening
1 egg, beaten
1 c. milk

In a large bowl, sift together dry ingredients. Cut in shortening with a pastry blender until mixture resembles coarse meal. Combine egg and milk in a separate bowl. Add to flour mixture all at once; stir with a fork just enough to make a soft dough that sticks together. Turn onto a lightly floured surface; knead gently 15 times. Roll to one-inch thickness. Cut with a floured 2-inch round biscuit cutter. Place biscuits one inch apart on an ungreased baking sheet. Bake at 450 degrees for 12 to 15 minutes, until golden. Makes 16 biscuits.

Southern Chocolate Gravy

Tina Butler
Mesquite, TX

My mother used to make chocolate gravy almost every weekend. My brothers, sister and I always got so excited to see the bowl of piping-hot chocolate gravy on the table with a big basket of biscuits! For sweeter gravy, you can increase the amount of sugar to 3/4 cup.

1/2 c. sugar
2 T. all-purpose flour
1 T. baking cocoa
1-1/4 c. milk

1 T. butter
1/2 t. vanilla extract
4 biscuits, split

Combine sugar, flour and cocoa in a saucepan. Whisk in milk. Bring to a boil over medium heat, then reduce heat, stirring constantly to prevent scorching. When gravy thickens, remove from heat; stir in butter and vanilla. Serve over warm biscuits. Makes 4 servings.

Appetizers & Snacks

Mini Ham & Swiss Frittatas

Celestina Torrez
Camden, NJ

I first started making these for my toddlers as easy-to-handle mini omelets. My husband thought they would be yummy as appetizers too, so now I serve them when we're watching the big game on TV. They're still a hit with my kids too!

8-oz. pkg. cooked ham, diced
2/3 c. shredded Swiss cheese
1/4 c. fresh chives, chopped

pepper to taste
3 T. butter, melted
8 eggs, beaten

In a bowl, mix together ham, cheese, chives and pepper; set aside. Brush mini muffin cups with melted butter. Fill muffin cups half full with cheese mixture. Spoon in eggs to fill cups. Bake at 375 degrees until golden, about 13 minutes. Serve warm. Makes 2 dozen.

Looking for a new way to serve a favorite snack?
Retro-style plates, cake stands and chip & dip sets
really add color and fun.

English Muffin Pizzas

JoAnna Nicoline-Haughey
Berwyn, PA

Back in the 1960s when I was growing up, my mom used to make these for us as an after-school snack. Add some pepperoni slices or other favorite toppings, if you like.

12-oz. pkg. English muffins, split

15-oz. can pizza sauce
2 c. shredded mozzarella cheese

Spread each muffin half with pizza sauce; sprinkle with cheese. Bake at 350 degrees for 10 minutes, or until cheese is melted. Makes 6 servings.

Whip up some fruit smoothies for a healthy snack. Fill a blender with your favorite fresh or frozen fruit...strawberries and peaches are especially luscious! Add fruit juice or yogurt to taste. Process until smooth and garnish with a sprig of fresh mint.

Good Times Veggie Pizza

Beckie Kreml
Peebles, OH

My mom used to make this quick appetizer for our church's fellowship on Sundays after the evening service. Everyone still loves it! Try cutting your pizza into bite-size squares for easy nibbling.

2 8-oz. tubes refrigerated
  crescent rolls
8-oz. pkg. cream cheese,
  softened
1-oz. pkg. ranch salad dressing
  mix
1 c. broccoli, finely chopped

1 c. carrots, peeled and diced
1 c. green peppers, diced
1/2 c. tomatoes, diced
1/2 c. lettuce, chopped
1 to 2 c. shredded Cheddar
  cheese

Roll out crescent roll dough onto an ungreased baking sheet. Press seams together to form a rectangle. Pinch together edges to form a crust. Bake at 375 minutes for 12 minutes; cool completely. Combine cream cheese and ranch dip. Spread over crust; top with vegetables, then cheese. Cover and refrigerate for at least an hour; cut into squares. Makes 16 servings.

Vintage game boards make whimsical settings for game night buffets!
Check the closet for forgotten games or pick some up at yard sales.
Cover with self-adhesive clear plastic for wipe-clean convenience.

Pepperoni Egg Rolls

Wendy Wright
New London, WI

*My mother made these for our family's annual football party
and they were such a hit...really different and tasty! Set out
a bowl of warmed pizza sauce for dipping.*

16-oz. pkg. egg roll wrappers
1 doz. pieces string cheese
8-oz. can pizza sauce

8-oz. pkg. sliced pepperoni
oil for deep frying

Lay out egg roll wrappers on a counter. Top each wrapper with a piece
of string cheese, 2 tablespoons pizza sauce and 4 pepperoni slices.
Roll up, tucking in the sides as you roll. In a deep fryer over high heat,
heat several inches oil to 375 degrees. Add egg rolls, a few at a time.
Cook for 2 to 3 minutes, or until golden. Remove with a slotted spoon.
Drain on paper towels; let cool before serving. Makes one dozen.

Lemony iced tea is so refreshing with snacks! Brew 9 teabags
in 3 quarts boiling water for 5 minutes. Discard teabags, then
stir in a 12-ounce can of frozen lemonade concentrate and
a cup of sugar. Chill; serve over ice cubes.

Rye Cocktail Rounds

Kelly Patrick
Ashburn, VA

My mom used to make these tasty little appetizers for parties. Dad couldn't resist sneaking a spoon into the topping mixture as it was warming up. It was so funny...he'd eat so much out of the pan that Mom never had quite enough to top all the little bread slices!

1 lb. ground beef	1 t. dried oregano
1 lb. mild ground pork sausage	1/2 t. garlic salt
1 lb. pasteurized process cheese	1/2 t. Worcestershire sauce
spread, cubed	1 loaf sliced party rye bread

Brown beef and sausage in a skillet over medium heat; drain. Add remaining ingredients except bread; mix well and stir until cheese is melted. Arrange bread slices on ungreased baking sheets. Spread with beef mixture. Bake at 350 degrees for 20 minutes. Rounds may be reheated in the oven as needed; cover with aluminum foil before reheating. Makes 2-1/2 dozen.

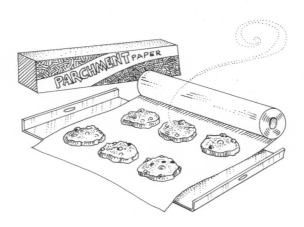

Sweet or savory treats won't stick to baking sheets lined with parchment paper. Clean-up is a snap too...just toss away the paper.

Cucumber Tea Sandwiches

Celeste Pierce
Overland Park, KS

I like to think I'm a good cook, but this simple recipe is the one people always request! These dainty sandwiches are one of the few things that my 89-year-old mother still has an appetite for.

2 cucumbers, peeled and thinly
   sliced
1 c. sour cream
1/2 c. mayonnaise
1 t. dill weed

1/2 t. onion powder
1/2 t. seasoned salt
1/4 t. garlic powder
1/8 t. kosher salt
20 slices white bread

Place cucumber slices between paper towels; allow to dry for
5 minutes. Mix together remaining ingredients except bread. Spread
sour cream mixture over one side of all 20 bread slices. Cover
10 slices with cucumbers; top with remaining bread slices. Quarter
each sandwich; arrange on a serving plate. Cover and refrigerate; best
served within 6 hours. Makes 40 servings.

Just for fun, spear cherry tomatoes, cheese cubes or tiny gherkin
pickles with a toothpick and use to fasten party sandwiches.

Best Beef Jerky

Amy Wrightsel
Louisville, KY

This recipe has become a family favorite for my boys...as soon as the weather turns chilly, they start asking when we will make jerky. It is very easy to make. You don't need any fancy tools, just everyday baking items that you probably have in your kitchen.

1-1/2 to 2 lbs. beef flank steak
2/3 c. Worcestershire sauce
2/3 c. soy sauce
1 T. honey

2 t. chili powder
2 t. onion powder
2 t. red pepper flakes
1 t. salt

With a sharp knife, slice beef against the grain into 1/4-inch thick strips. Combine remaining ingredients in a large, wide bowl; add beef strips. Cover and refrigerate overnight, turning beef strips occasionally. The next morning, preheat oven to its lowest setting, 145 to 160 degrees. Line 2 baking sheets with aluminum foil; top each with a heavy wire rack. Drain beef strips; discard marinade. Pat strips dry and arrange on the racks evenly, without touching. Place in oven, leaving the door open slightly for air circulation. Bake at lowest oven setting until dry but still firm, about 10 to 12 hours, turning once or twice. Once dry, store in a cool dry place, in an airtight container for 2 to 3 months. Makes 4 to 6 servings.

Pack a snack and go on a nature walk...crunchy snack mix or chewy jerky are perfect. Be sure to take along a pocket-size nature guide, a magnifying glass and a tote bag to bring back special finds...you'll have as much fun as the kids do!

Appetizers & Snacks

Bacon-Wrapped Smokies

Sheila Roemer
Red Cloud, NE

*My grandmother makes this recipe and it's one of my favorites too.
I took them once to our church dinner and had so many compliments.
They are really tasty and so easy to pick up and go.*

1 lb. bacon
14-oz. pkg. mini smoked
   sausages

1/2 c. brown sugar, packed

Cut bacon slices in half and arrange on an ungreased baking sheet.
Bake at 350 degrees for about 20 minutes, or until cooked but not
crisp. Remove from oven; cool slightly and drain. Wrap each mini
sausage in a bacon slice; secure with wooden toothpicks. Return to
baking sheet and sprinkle with brown sugar. Bake, uncovered, at
350 degrees for about 20 minutes, until bacon is crisp. Makes about
3-1/2 dozen.

Put out the welcome mat and invite friends over for a
retro-style appetizer party. Serve up yummy finger foods
like Bacon-Wrapped Smokies and play favorite tunes from
the 1950s or 1960s...everyone is sure to have a blast!

Teddy Bear Honey Munchies

Abby Bills
Orleans, NE

A fun summertime snack for kids...they can even help make it!

3-oz. pkg. ramen noodles
5 c. bite-size sweetened graham
   cereal squares
3 c. bear-shaped graham
   crackers
1 c. dry-roasted peanuts

1 c. raisins
1/3 c. butter
1/3 c. honey
1 t. orange juice
1/2 t. cinnamon

Crush ramen noodles; reserve seasoning packet for another use. In a large bowl, toss together noodles, cereal, crackers, peanuts and raisins. Combine remaining ingredients in a microwave-safe cup. Microwave on high, stirring after 15-second intervals, until well mixed and butter is melted. Pour over noodle mixture; toss to coat well. Spread onto ungreased rimmed baking sheets. Bake at 375 degrees for 10 minutes, stirring once. Cool before serving; store in an airtight container. Makes 15 servings.

When a snack mix recipe makes a lot of servings, spoon it into a nostalgic metal lunchbox along with a scoop. A stack of snack-size paper bags nearby will make it easy for everyone to help themselves.

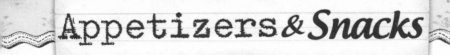

Hannah's Sweet Snack Mix

Katie Majeske
Denver, PA

When my daughter, Hannah, was little, this was one of her very favorite treats. She often took it to school for her snack and would request it for almost all her birthday parties. She even shared her version of it in a recipe book that her kindergarten teacher put together.

18-oz. pkg. plain fish-shaped
    crackers
1 c. dry-roasted peanuts
1 c. sugar

1/2 c. light corn syrup
1/2 c. butter
1 t. vanilla extract
1 t. baking soda

In a large bowl, toss together crackers and peanuts; set aside. In a saucepan over medium heat, combine sugar, corn syrup and butter. Bring to a boil; boil for 5 minutes. Remove from heat; stir in vanilla and baking soda. Pour sugar mixture over cracker mixture; stir to coat. Spread onto ungreased rimmed baking sheets. Bake, uncovered, at 250 degrees for one hour, stirring every 15 minutes. Cool on wax paper; break into bite-size pieces. Store in an airtight container. Makes 12 servings.

Peanuts are yummy in crunchy snack mixes, but if you need to avoid them, there are tasty substitutes to try! Choose from raisins, sweetened dried cranberries, dried fruit bits, cereal squares, candy-coated chocolates, regular or white chocolate chips and even mini pretzel twists.

Grandmother's Ham Spread

Barbara Klein
Newburgh, IN

This recipe was handed down from my grandmother. My mother would make this recipe every time we bought a ham. It makes the best cold sandwiches...grilled sandwiches too! It is also very good served on crisp crackers as an appetizer.

8-oz. can tomato sauce
2 T. catsup
1 T. mustard
1 t. Worcestershire sauce
1 t. vinegar

2 T. instant tapioca, uncooked
1 lb. pasteurized process cheese
   spread, cubed
3 lbs. smoked ham, boiled
   and ground

In a stockpot over medium heat, combine all ingredients except cheese and ham. Cook and stir just until thickened. Remove from heat; add cheese. When cheese is melted, add ham and mix thoroughly. Chill before serving. Makes 20 servings.

An old-fashioned food grinder is handy for grinding meat for spreads, meatloaf and other recipes. To clean it easily when you've finished, just put a half-slice of bread through the grinder. The bread will remove any food particles.

Smoky Salmon Spread

Kay Snyder
Cuba, NY

My dad would be so proud that I'm sharing this flavorful recipe!
You can use it as a dip or spread it on crackers.

16-oz. can salmon, drained
8-oz. pkg. cream cheese,
   softened
2 T. lemon juice
2 T. prepared horseradish

1 T. onion, grated
1/2 to 1 t. smoke-flavored
   cooking sauce
1/4 t. salt
1/4 c. pistachios, finely chopped

Flake salmon, discarding any skin or bones. Combine all ingredients
in a large bowl and mix thoroughly. Refrigerate for several hours
before serving. Makes about 2 cups.

Scoop out the centers of cherry tomatoes and thick slices of cucumber,
then fill with a dollop of a flavorful, creamy spread. Lighter than
crackers and chips...so pretty on an appetizer tray too!

Crispy Chicken Tasties

Kelly Korokis
Fredericktown, MO

*My mom makes these appetizers for everything from family
dinners to snacking while watching sports on television.
We love 'em...they're even good cold!*

1/2 c. lemon juice
3 T. soy sauce
1/2 t. salt
3 lbs. boneless, skinless chicken
    breasts, cut into 1-inch cubes

1 c. all-purpose flour.
1 T. pepper
1/2 t. salt
1 T. paprika
peanut oil for frying

Mix lemon juice, soy sauce and salt together in a large bowl. Add
chicken. Refrigerate for 3 hours, stirring occasionally. Drain,
discarding marinade. Combine remaining ingredients except oil in a
separate bowl. Coat chicken in flour mixture. Heat oil in a large skillet
over medium-high heat. Add chicken; cook until golden on all sides
and chicken juices run clear. Drain on paper towels before serving.
Makes 6 to 8 servings.

Making some yummy deviled eggs for a party or picnic?
Whip 'em up in no time by spooning the egg yolk filling into
a plastic zipping bag. Snip off a corner and pipe the filling
into the egg white halves...simple!

Sassy Hot Wings

Paula Marchesi
Lenhartsville, PA

Our family really likes hot chicken wings! After ordering out and searching in vain for a good recipe, I finally decided to come up with my own. It is simply delicious!

1/2 c. butter, sliced	2 T. plus 1 t. celery seed, divided
1/2 c. hot pepper sauce	2/3 c. all-purpose flour
1/4 c. balsamic vinegar	1 t. seasoned salt
1/4 c. soy sauce	1 t. paprika
3 T. brown sugar, packed	1 t. cayenne pepper
2 T. lemon juice	1/2 t. garlic powder
1-1/2 T. maple syrup	5 lbs. chicken wings
1-1/2 T. honey	oil for frying

In a saucepan, combine butter, hot sauce, vinegar, soy sauce, brown sugar, lemon juice, maple syrup, honey and 2 tablespoons celery seed. Bring to a boil over medium heat. Reduce heat and simmer, uncovered, until reduced by half; set aside. Meanwhile, in a large plastic zipping bag, combine flour, seasonings and remaining celery seed. Add wings to bag, a few at a time, and shake to coat. In an electric skillet or deep fryer, heat several inches of oil to 375 degrees. Fry wings, a few at a time, for 6 to 8 minutes each, or until juices run clear when pierced, turning once. Drain on paper towels. Place wings in a large bowl; add warm sauce and toss to coat. Makes about 4 dozen.

A tray of warm, moistened towels is a must when serving sticky barbecue ribs or chicken wings! Dampen fingertip towels in water and a dash of lemon juice, roll up and microwave on high for 10 to 15 seconds.

Honey-Rum Pretzels

Rebekah Tank
Mount Calvary, WI

I think this crunchy snack is even better than caramel corn! It is so easy to make and always disappears fast. If you prefer, you can eliminate the rum extract and double the maple extract.

1/2 c. brown sugar, packed
1/4 c. butter, sliced
1 T. honey
1/4 t. salt

1/4 t. baking soda
1/8 t. rum extract
1/8 t. maple extract
6 c. mini twist pretzels

In a large microwave-safe bowl, combine brown sugar, butter and honey. Microwave on high for 45 seconds to one minute, until butter melts. Stir; microwave about 30 seconds longer, until mixture boils. Immediately stir in salt, baking soda and extracts. Stir in pretzels. Microwave for 20 to 30 seconds. Stir until well coated. Spread on wax paper. Cool before serving. Makes 6 to 8 cups.

Playful Pretzels

Lisa Fassett
Burlington Flats, NY

My grandchildren and I enjoy making these pretzels together. They can be formed into any shape, either by hand or using cookie cutters.

1 env. active dry yeast
1-1/4 c. warm water
4 c. all-purpose flour

1 t. salt
1 T. sugar
Garnish: butter, cinnamon-sugar

In a large bowl, dissolve yeast in very warm water, 110 to 115 degrees. Add flour, salt and sugar; mix well. Form dough as desired; place on lightly greased baking sheets. Garnish as desired. Bake at 425 degrees for 12 to 15 minutes. Makes about 2 dozen.

Porch Popcorn

Barb Bargdill
Gooseberry Patch

A family favorite! When my kids were little, they really looked forward to making this as soon as it turned cold outside. They loved putting the bowl on the porch and then waiting by the door until the chocolate-coated popcorn was set enough for them to eat.

1 lb. melting chocolate, chopped
1/4 c. creamy peanut butter
12 to 16 c. salted popped
   popcorn

1-1/2 c. salted peanuts
1-1/2 c. crispy rice cereal

Place chocolate in a microwave-safe bowl. Microwave on high for one minute; stir. Add peanut butter; microwave an additional one to 2 minutes, until chocolate is completely melted. Stir mixture until creamy. Place popcorn in a large bowl or roasting pan; drizzle half the chocolate mixture over popcorn and stir. Sprinkle in peanuts and cereal, stirring to mix well. Pour remaining chocolate mixture over all; stir gently to coat. Spread onto parchment paper-lined baking sheets. Put on a cool porch or in the refrigerator until chocolate is hardened. Break up any large pieces before serving. Store in an airtight container. Makes about 16 to 20 cups.

Share laughs during a family movie night...bring out the home movies of when Mom & Dad were kids. Or share feature films that were extra-special to you when you were growing up. Pass the popcorn, please!

Spinach-Artichoke Dip

Diane Cohen
The Woodlands, TX

I've been making this yummy dip for get-togethers for years.

2 8-oz. pkgs. cream cheese,
  softened
1/2 c. mayonnaise
14-oz. can artichoke hearts,
  drained and chopped
10-oz. pkg. frozen chopped
  spinach, thawed and drained

1/2 c. grated Parmesan cheese
1 clove garlic, minced
snack crackers, cut-up
  vegetables

Place cream cheese and mayonnaise in a bowl. Beat with an electric mixer on medium speed until well blended. Add remaining ingredients except crackers and vegetables; mix well. Transfer mixture to a greased 9" pie plate. Bake, uncovered, at 350 degrees for 20 to 25 minutes, until lightly golden. Serve with crackers or vegetables. Makes 16 servings.

A quick and tasty appetizer in a jiffy...place a block of cream cheese on a serving plate, spoon sweet-hot pepper jelly over it and serve with crunchy crackers.

Marinated Garlic Olives

Sharon Velenosi
Stanton, CA

A few simple ingredients can do wonders for ordinary canned olives...you'll be amazed at the flavor!

2 c. green olives, drained
1 to 2 cloves garlic, slivered
3 thin slices lemon
1 t. whole peppercorns

3 bay leaves
1/4 c. wine vinegar
1/4 to 1/2 c. olive oil

In a wide-mouthed jar with a lid, combine all ingredients except oil. Add enough oil to cover ingredients. Secure lid. Refrigerate at least 24 hours to blend flavors before serving. Makes 2 cups.

Serving appetizers before dinner? Offer small bites like Marinated Garlic Olives that will sharpen guests' appetites but not fill them up.

Golden Onion Rings

Wendy Jacobs
Idaho Falls, ID

Serve with ranch dressing for dipping...yum!

2-1/2 c. all-purpose flour
2 t. baking powder
2 t. salt
2 onions, sliced and separated
   into rings

2 eggs, beaten
2 c. milk
1-1/2 c. dry bread crumbs
oil for deep frying
salt and pepper to taste

Stir together flour, baking powder and salt. Coat onion rings with mixture; set aside. Whisk eggs and milk into remaining flour mixture. Dip floured onion rings into mixture. Drain on a wire rack; coat with bread crumbs. In a large saucepan, heat several inches oil to 375 degrees. Fry onion rings, a few at a time, until golden, 2 to 3 minutes each. Drain on paper towels. Sprinkle with salt and pepper; serve warm. Serves 6.

My mother had a great deal of trouble with me,
but I think she enjoyed it.

-Mark Twain

Appetizers & *Snacks*

Sensational Hot Sausage Dip

Jessica Haynes
Salem, WV

*Both my husband's family and my own request this appetizer
at every family function...my friends ask for it too!*

1 lb. hot ground pork sausage
1 lb. medium ground pork
    sausage
2 8-oz. pkgs. cream cheese,
    softened

1 onion, finely chopped
4 Anaheim chili peppers, finely
    chopped
tortilla chips or wheat crackers

Brown sausage in a skillet over medium heat; drain. In a bowl,
combine cream cheese, onion and peppers. Add sausage and mix well.
Place in an ungreased 2-quart casserole dish. Bake, uncovered, at
350 degrees for 30 minutes, until top is slightly golden. Serve warm
with tortilla chips or crackers. Makes 36 servings.

Crunchy Wheat Crackers

Marian Buckley
Fontana, CA

Use a serrated pastry wheel to cut the crackers...so fancy!

1-1/2 c. all-purpose flour
1/2 c. whole-wheat flour
1/2 c. sugar
1/4 t. salt

2 T. butter
1/2 to 2/3 c. milk
coarse salt to taste

In a bowl, combine flours, sugar and salt. Cut in butter until mixture
resembles coarse meal. Blend in milk gradually until dough forms.
Divide dough into 2 parts. On a floured surface, roll out each part
1/8-inch thick. Sprinkle with salt; press salt gently into dough. Cut
into 2-inch by 2-inch squares; place on ungreased baking sheets.
Bake at 325 degrees for 20 to 25 minutes, until lightly golden. Cool;
store in an airtight container. Makes about 9 dozen.

Sweet Apple Dip

Lori Peterson
Effingham, KS

Kids will love eating fresh apples with this creamy brown sugar dip. Its flavor is even better the second day.

8-oz. pkg. cream cheese,
   softened
3/4 c. brown sugar, packed

1/4 c. sugar
1 t. vanilla extract
apple slices

In a bowl, blend together all ingredients except apples. Serve with apple slices. Serve immediately or chill; refrigerate any leftovers. Serves 10.

You may know that lemon juice keeps apple slices from browning, but in a pinch, you can use lemon-lime soda.

Marshmallow Fruit Dip

Kris Thompson
Ripley, NY

A good friend used to bring this to our potlucks at work. Now I make it for family & friends. It's scrumptious with juicy ripe strawberries, pineapple cubes, grapes and other fruit.

8-oz. pkg. cream cheese,
   softened
2 7-oz. jars marshmallow creme

1 t. vanilla extract
assorted fruit slices and cubes

In a large bowl, beat cream cheese until smooth. Add marshmallow creme and vanilla; beat until smooth. Serve with assorted fruits. Refrigerate any leftovers. Makes 8 servings.

Need a quick, good-for-you after-school snack? Serve up an old favorite, Ants on a Log...celery sticks filled with peanut butter and sprinkled with raisins. Kids can even substitute sweetened dried cranberries to make Fire Ants on a Log...fun and tasty!

Warm Crab Puffs

Nancy Gasko
South Bend, IN

I've enjoyed cooking since I was a little girl. Teaching my daughter and now my grandchildren to cook has been a great joy for me.

6-oz. can crabmeat, drained
1/2 c. butter, softened
5-oz. jar sharp pasteurized
    process cheese spread

6 English muffins, split

Mix crabmeat, butter and cheese well. Spread on split English muffins. Cut muffins into quarters; place on ungreased baking sheets and freeze overnight. Remove and place puffs in a plastic freezer bag. Place frozen puffs on ungreased baking sheets; bake at 400 degrees for 5 to 10 minutes, until puffy and golden. Puffs may be stored in the freezer for several months before baking. Makes 2 dozen.

A punch bowl is a festive touch that makes even the simplest party beverage special! Surround it with a wreath of fresh flowers or bunches of grapes.

Yummy Spinach Balls

Kelly Wilkie
Garnet Valley, PA

These savory warm spinach bites are always a hit at parties.

10-oz. pkg. frozen chopped
   spinach, thawed and drained
6-oz. pkg. herb-flavored stuffing
   mix
5 eggs, beaten

1 onion, chopped
1/2 c. butter, melted
1/2 t. pepper
1/4 t. garlic powder
1/4 t. dried thyme

In a bowl, mix all ingredients well. Form into one to 1-1/2 inch balls.
Place on an ungreased baking sheet; freeze for at least 30 minutes,
until firm. Remove from freezer and place on well-greased baking
sheets. Bake, uncovered, at 375 degrees for 25 minutes, or until
lightly golden. Spinach balls may be stored in plastic freezer bags up
to one month; bake at serving time. Makes 15 to 20 servings.

Stock up on festive party napkins, plates and candles at
post-holiday sales. Tuck them away in a big box...you'll be all set
to turn any casual meal or get-together into a party!

Anytime Ham Dip

Cheryl Baker
Houston, TX

I have been making this dip for over thirty years. When my kids were little, they called it "Mommy Dip." It tastes terrific with chips or fresh veggies, and with only three ingredients, it is so easy!

12-oz. container whipped cream
   cheese
4-1/4 oz. can deviled ham
   spread

1/2 c. sour cream

Mix all ingredients and serve. Keep refrigerated. Serves 10 to 15.

A crockery bowl filled to the brim with ripe pears, apples and other fresh fruit makes an oh-so-simple centerpiece...it's a great way to encourage healthy snacking too!

Flavor Craver Shrimp Dip

Pamela Stanley
Portsmouth, NH

*My Aunt Carol gave me this recipe years ago, and it has been a
hit at parties ever since! It's really tasty served with scoop-type
corn chips, potato chips and carrot and celery sticks.*

1/2 c. chili sauce
8-oz. pkg. cream cheese,
   softened
1/2 c. mayonnaise

1/3 c. onion, chopped
2 t. prepared horseradish
4-1/2 oz. can tiny shrimp,
   rinsed and drained

Blend chili sauce gradually into cream cheese. Mix in mayonnaise,
onion and horseradish; fold in shrimp. Cover and chill at least one
hour. Makes 2-1/2 cups.

Microwave Potato Chips

Nancy Wise
Little Rock, AR

*Yum...you'll never go back to store-bought chips! Try adding
seasoned salt, smoked pepper or other seasonings too.*

3 T. oil
3 potatoes, peeled and very
   thinly sliced

salt to taste

Pour oil into a plastic zipping bag; add potato slices and shake to coat.
Coat a large microwave-safe plate with non-stick vegetable spray.
Arrange potato slices on plate in a single layer. Microwave on high for
3 to 5 minutes, until crisp and lightly golden. Remove chips to a paper
towel; sprinkle with salt. Repeat with remaining potatoes. Serves 4 to 6.

Colorful, fresh veggies are always welcome at parties and easy to
prepare in advance. Cut them into bite-size slices, flowerets or cubes
and tuck away in plastic zipping bags until needed...what a time-saver!

Grass Granola

Leona Krivda
Belle Vernon, PA

My children and grandchildren love to munch on this sweet, crunchy granola by the handful...I love how easy it is to make!

4 c. long-cooking oats,
  uncooked
1/3 c. untoasted wheat germ
1/3 c. sesame seed
1/3 c. chopped walnuts

1/4 c. honey
1/4 c. butter, melted
1/2 t. cinnamon
1/2 c. sweetened dried
  cranberries

In a large bowl, mix together oats, wheat germ, sesame seed and walnuts. In a separate bowl, combine honey, butter and cinnamon. Add honey mixture to oat mixture and mix well. Spread on ungreased baking sheets in a thin layer. Bake at 350 degrees for 15 to 20 minutes, stirring every 5 minutes. Cool completely; stir in cranberries. Store in an airtight container. Makes about 5 cups.

Brightly colored new beach pails make whimsical servers for chips and snacks...use a sand shovel as a serving scoop!

Mom's Puppy Chow

Shonnie Sims
Canton, GA

*My mom always made this tasty snack in the fall...it still reminds me
of cool weather and spending time with family.*

16-oz. pkg. bite-size crispy corn
   cereal squares
1 c. sugar

1 c. corn syrup
1 c. creamy peanut butter
1 c. dry-roasted peanuts

Place cereal in a large bowl; set aside. In a microwave-safe bowl,
combine sugar, corn syrup and peanut butter. Microwave on high until
melted, about 3 minutes. Add peanuts; mix well and pour over cereal.
Toss evenly to coat. Store in an airtight container. Makes 10 servings.

Mom's Surprise Chocolate Toffee

Jewel Sharpe
Raleigh, NC

*My mom made this candylike treat often...it is so good! It's fun
to see if anyone guesses that they're made from saltines.*

1 sleeve saltine crackers
1 c. butter
1 c. light brown sugar, packed

1/2 c. mini semi-sweet chocolate
   chips
1/2 c. chopped pecans

Line a 15"x10" jelly-roll pan with aluminum foil. Arrange saltines in
a single layer on pan. In a microwave-safe bowl, microwave butter
and brown sugar on high for 4 minutes, or until hot and bubbly. Stir
well and pour evenly over saltines. Sprinkle with chocolate chips and
pecans. Bake at 275 degrees for about 12 minutes. Cool completely;
break apart. Makes about 20 servings.

A vintage hand-cranked mini food chopper quickly chops small
quantities of nuts for snacks, desserts and other recipes.

Cheri's Chicken Nuggets

Cheri Maxwell
Gulf Breeze, FL

Terrific for easy weeknight meals or parties! Serve with your favorite dipping sauce.

1/2 c. butter, melted
1 c. dry bread crumbs
1/2 c. grated Parmesan cheese
1 t. garlic salt

salt and pepper to taste
3 boneless, skinless chicken
  breasts, cut into strips

Place melted butter in a bowl. In a separate bowl, mix together bread crumbs, cheese and seasonings. Dip chicken into butter, then into bread crumb mixture. Place chicken in a single layer on a lightly greased baking sheet. Bake at 400 degrees for 20 minutes, or until juices run clear when pierced. Makes 4 to 6 servings.

Good-on-Anything BBQ Sauce

Jill Webb
Christiansburg, VA

My husband loves this sauce and we use it on everything! It's a combination of my mom's original recipe plus ingredients I added to create the perfect blend.

2 c. catsup
1 c. water
1/4 c. cider vinegar
1/4 c. molasses
1/2 c. brown sugar, packed
1/4 c. sugar

1 T. mustard
1 t. dry mustard
1 t. onion powder
1 t. chili powder
2 to 3 cloves garlic, minced

In a saucepan over medium heat, whisk all ingredients together. Cook until mixture starts to bubble and thickens slightly. Use immediately or refrigerate. Makes 4 cups.

Soups, Bread
&Sandwiches

Love
Mom

Little Pigs in a Mud Hole

Lisa Engwell
Bellevue, NE

My dad's recipe for simple down-home comfort food...whenever we visit my parents, they make sure to have it simmering in the slow cooker! When my brother and I were growing up, money was tight and this was economical. Dad gave it this clever name to get us to try it. He made it with ham hocks, and the little sausages are my addition. Serve with cornbread...yum!

16-oz. pkg. mixed dried beans
1 to 2 14-oz. pkgs. mini
   smoked sausages
1 onion, diced
32-oz. container chicken broth
12 to 15 c. water

1 T. garlic, minced
chili powder, salt and pepper
   to taste
Optional: 3 to 4 pickled hot
   peppers, chopped
cooked rice

Rinse beans in a colander; place in a 6-quart slow-cooker. Add sausages, onion, broth and enough water to fill slow cooker. Stir in remaining ingredients except rice. Cover and cook on high setting for 6 to 8 hours. Serve with rice. Serves 6 to 8.

Soup suppers are a fuss-free way to get together with friends, neighbors and family. Each family brings a favorite soup to share, along with the recipe...you provide the bowls, spoons and a super-simple dessert like brownies. What a delicious way to try a variety of soups and maybe find a new favorite!

Soups, Breads & *Sandwiches*

Cowboy Cornbread

Ruth Cooksey
Plainfield, IN

*When this delicious cornbread was served at a luncheon
at our apartment clubhouse, it was the talk of the party!
Try it yourself...you'll agree!*

2 c. biscuit baking mix
1 c. yellow cornmeal
1-1/2 t. baking powder
1/2 t. salt
3/4 c. sugar

2 eggs, beaten
1 c. half-and-half
1 c. butter, melted and slightly
   cooled

In a bowl, mix together dry ingredients. Add remaining ingredients;
stir until well blended. Pour into a greased 13"x9" baking pan. Bake
at 350 degrees for 25 to 30 minutes. Cut into squares. Makes about
12 servings.

Thinking of a menu for guests? Let the season be your guide! Soups
and stews chock-full of harvest's bounty are just right for fall
get-togethers, and juicy fruit salads are delightful in the summer.
Not only will you get the freshest ingredients when you plan
by the season, you'll get the best prices at the supermarket!

Irish Spud Soup

Kyle Fugate
Newburgh, IN

My kids can't wait for the weather to get colder so they can curl up with a steaming bowl of this scrumptious potato soup.

2 T. butter
2 c. onion, chopped
1 c. celery, chopped
1 t. garlic, minced
8 c. chicken broth
3-1/2 lbs. potatoes, peeled and cubed

2 c. shredded Cheddar cheese
1 c. green onion, chopped
1-1/2 t. salt
1 t. pepper
Garnish: shredded Cheddar cheese, sliced green onion

Melt butter in a stockpot over medium heat. Add onion, celery and garlic. Cook for 4 minutes, or until vegetables are softened. Add broth and potatoes; bring to a boil. Reduce heat to low. Simmer, uncovered, for about 45 minutes, stirring occasionally, or until soup is thick and only small chunks of potato remain. Add remaining ingredients except garnish; stir until cheese melts. Garnish as desired. Serves 8.

Take the kids to a paint-your-own pottery shop! Let them decorate cheery soup bowls for the whole family. Their creations will warm hearts and tummies at the same time.

Spicy Potato Soup

Janice Gavarkavich
Martins Ferry, OH

My daughter, who's now twenty-five, loves this soup. She always liked chili, but hated the beans...this was perfect for her! She took a copy of the recipe with her recently when she got married. Diced celery and carrots are a tasty addition.

1 lb. ground beef
1 onion, chopped
1 green pepper, finely chopped
4 c. potatoes, peeled and cubed
3 8-oz. cans tomato sauce

5 c. water
2 t. salt
1-1/2 t. pepper
1/2 to 1 t. hot pepper sauce

In a Dutch oven over medium heat, brown beef, onion and green pepper; drain. Stir in remaining ingredients; bring to a boil. Reduce heat to low. Cover and simmer for one hour, stirring occasionally, or until potatoes are tender and soup has thickened. Makes 6 servings.

Keep a cherished cookbook clean and free of spatters. Slip it into a gallon-size plastic zipping bag before cooking up a favorite recipe.

Mom's Champion Chicken Soup

Melody Taynor
Everett, WA

Guaranteed to chase away the chills! For extra goodness,
use homemade chicken broth...you'll need about 10 cups.

1 T. butter
1/2 c. onion, chopped
1/2 c. celery, chopped
2 32-oz. containers chicken
   broth
14-1/2 oz. can chicken broth

1 c. cooked chicken, diced
1 c. carrots, peeled and sliced
2 t. dried parsley
salt and pepper to taste
1-1/2 c. thin egg noodles,
   uncooked

Melt butter in a stockpot over medium heat. Sauté onion and celery in butter until just tender, about 5 minutes. Pour in broth; add remaining ingredients except noodles. Bring to a boil; stir in noodles. Reduce heat slightly and simmer for 15 to 20 minutes, until noodles are tender. Makes 6 servings.

Welcoming extra guests for dinner? It's easy to stretch a pot of soup to make more servings. Check the pantry for quick-cooking instant rice or ramen noodles...add an extra can or two of veggies. The soup will be extra hearty and no one will know the difference.

Chicken Tortilla Soup

Amber Mayfield
Fort Walton Beach, FL

My husband and daughter really like this soup...it's so yummy and simple to make, I'm happy to prepare it for them!

4 c. chicken broth
2 c. cooked chicken, diced
2 15-oz. cans diced tomatoes,
    drained
16-oz. can corn, drained
16-oz. can pinto or red beans,
    drained and rinsed

1-1/3 c. salsa
2 T. taco seasoning mix
Garnish: sour cream, shredded
    Mexican-blend cheese, corn
    or tortilla chips

Combine all ingredients except garnish in a stockpot over medium heat. Simmer, covered, for 30 minutes, stirring occasionally. Top individual portions with desired garnishes. Serves 6 to 8.

While the soup is simmering, make some crunchy tortilla strip toppers. Brush or spray olive oil over both sides of flour tortillas. Cut the tortillas into narrow strips and place on a baking sheet. Bake at 375 degrees for 5 to 7 minutes, turning once or twice, until crisp and golden.

Slow-Cooked Veggie-Beef Soup

Pat Beach
Fisherville, KY

For someone who couldn't even boil water when she got married, my daughter, Toni, is a fabulous cook! She fixes a hearty meal most nights for her family of six. She says all it takes to be a great cook is a good full-flavored recipe like this one.

1 to 1-1/2 lbs. stew beef, cubed
46-oz. can cocktail vegetable
   juice
2 c. water
5 cubes beef bouillon
1/2 onion, chopped

2 to 3 potatoes, peeled and
   cubed
3 c. cabbage, shredded
16-oz. pkg. frozen mixed
   vegetables

Place all ingredients in a large slow cooker. Cover and cook on low setting for about 9 hours, until all ingredients are tender. Makes 10 to 12 servings.

Herbed Bread Sticks

Anne Marie Smith
Rocky River, OH

These are tasty with hot soup...a "souper" way to use day-old buns!

8 hot dog buns
1/2 c. butter, softened
1 t. dried basil, crushed

1/2 t. garlic salt
1/4 t. dried parsley

Split buns in quarters, lengthwise. Blend remaining ingredients; spread over cut sides of buns. Place buns on an ungreased baking sheet. Bake at 300 degrees for about an hour, or until crisp and lightly golden. Store in a covered container. Makes about 2-1/2 dozen.

Fix watery soup in a jiffy...thicken it with just a sprinkling
of instant potato flakes. Works like a charm!

Stuffed Pepper Soup

Marian Muder
Hubbard, OH

My mother-in-law shared this recipe. It tastes just like stuffed green peppers...delicious made with garden-fresh peppers!

1-1/2 lbs. ground beef
2 to 3 T. margarine
2-1/2 c. beef broth
2 10-3/4 oz. cans tomato soup
15-oz. can diced tomatoes
1 onion, chopped

2 stalks celery, chopped
2 green peppers, chopped
2 cloves garlic, diced
1/8 t. sugar
salt and pepper to taste
1 c. cooked rice

In a stockpot over medium heat, brown beef in margarine; drain. Add remaining ingredients except rice; mix well. Reduce heat to low; cover and simmer for 45 minutes. Stir in rice and simmer an additional 15 minutes. Makes 10 to 12 servings.

Mix up your own salt-free herb seasoning. Fill a shaker-top jar with 2 teaspoons of garlic powder and a teaspoon each of onion powder, dry mustard, paprika, pepper, dried thyme and celery seed. Add a little cayenne pepper for spiciness. Terrific in soups and on veggies!

Vegetarian 3-Bean Chili

Lorrie Coop
Munday, TX

My daughter, who's a vegetarian, and I developed this recipe because we were having trouble finding foods she liked. It's become a favorite of hers. Give it a try...you'll never miss the meat!

1 onion, diced
1 c. green pepper, diced and
    divided
1 T. oil
15-oz. can chili beans
15-oz. can Great Northern
    beans, drained and rinsed
15-oz. can black beans, drained
    and rinsed

15-oz. can diced tomatoes
1-1/4 oz. pkg. taco seasoning
    mix
1-oz. pkg. ranch salad dressing
    mix
Garnish: sour cream, finely
    shredded mild Cheddar
    cheese

In a stockpot over medium heat, sauté onion and 3/4 cup green pepper in oil until tender, about 8 minutes. Drain; add remaining ingredients except garnish. Reduce heat; cover and simmer for one hour, stirring occasionally. Spoon into soup bowls; garnish with sour cream, shredded cheese and remaining green pepper. Serves 6.

Red-Hot Crackers

Lori Comer
Kernersville, NC

At the school where I work, our Home Ec teacher fixed these and placed them in the teachers' lounge. Everyone gobbled them up!

16-oz. pkg. saltine crackers
.4-oz. pkg. ranch salad dressing
    mix

2-1/2 T. red pepper flakes
1-1/2 c. canola oil

Arrange crackers in a single layer on ungreased baking sheets. Mix together remaining ingredients; drizzle over crackers. Let stand 2 to 3 hours. Break crackers apart and store in an airtight container. Makes 30 servings.

"Mom, It's Good" Chili

Mary Baker
Fountain, NC

My two picky teenagers seldom comment on anything
I cook...but this chili was a real winner!

2 lbs. ground beef
2 onions, chopped
2 green peppers, chopped
2 16-oz. cans kidney beans,
    drained and rinsed
2 16-oz. cans pinto beans,
    drained and rinsed
2 15-oz. cans diced tomatoes

15-oz. can diced tomatoes with
    green chiles
2 6-oz. cans tomato paste
2 T. chili powder
2 T. salt
Optional: 3 to 4 c. water
Garnish: shredded Cheddar
    cheese

In a stockpot, brown beef over medium heat; drain. Add other ingredients except water and cheese. Reduce heat to low; cover and simmer for 3 hours, stirring occasionally. If needed, add water to desired thickness. Serve topped with cheese. Makes 12 servings.

You can't have too much chili! Freeze leftovers in small containers, to be microwaved and spooned over hot dogs or baked potatoes for a quick & hearty lunch.

Potato & Celery Soup with Eggs

Julia Spiegelmeyer
Elizabethtown, PA

When I was a child, it really made my day whenever
Mom cooked up a pot of this delicious soup.

2 c. potatoes, peeled and diced
1 onion, diced
3 c. water
1 t. salt
1 t. pepper
1/4 c. celery, chopped

2 T. butter
3 eggs, hard-boiled, peeled
   and chopped
4 c. milk
1 T. fresh parsley, chopped

In a large pot over medium-high heat, combine potatoes, onion, water, salt and pepper. Bring to a boil; boil for 8 to 10 minutes. Add celery and cook an additional 5 to 10 minutes, until potatoes are soft. Stir in remaining ingredients and heat through. Serves 4 to 6.

Copy tried & true recipes onto file cards and have them laminated at a copying store. Punch a hole in the upper left corner and thread cards onto a key ring...now you can hang them on the fridge and they'll always be handy!

Polka-Dot Chowder

Lisa Sims
Martinsburg, WV

My stepmother introduced this slow-cooker recipe to me.
I've shared it with my family and everyone loves it!

16-oz. pkg. beef hot dogs, sliced
6 c. potatoes, peeled and cubed
1 onion, diced
2 15-1/4 oz. cans corn

3 T. butter
salt and pepper to taste
13-oz. can evaporated milk
Optional: seasoned salt

In a slow cooker, combine all ingredients except evaporated milk. Cover and cook on high setting for 3 hours and 40 minutes. Stir in evaporated milk. Cover and cook an additional 20 minutes before serving. Garnish portions with a sprinkle of seasoned salt, if desired. Serves 4 to 6.

Making butter is fun for kids. Pour a pint of heavy cream
into a chilled wide-mouth jar, cap the jar tightly and take turns
shaking until you see butter begin to form. When it's done,
uncap the jar and rinse the butter lightly with cool water.
Enjoy on warm, fresh-baked bread...yum!

Tomato-Tortellini Soup

*Amy Cooper
Lebanon, MO*

Mom enjoyed this soup at a restaurant. She began to experiment and came up with her own version...we think it's even better!

12-oz. pkg. frozen cheese
   tortellini, uncooked
28-oz. can crushed tomatoes
28-oz. can Italian-style diced
   tomatoes
6-oz. can tomato paste

2 c. half-and-half
1 c. milk
1 t. kosher salt
1 T. pepper, or to taste
Garnish: grated Parmesan
   cheese

Fill a stockpot with water; bring to a rolling boil over medium-high heat. Add tortellini; return to a boil. Remove from heat and let stand until tortellini float, 15 to 20 minutes; drain. Meanwhile, in a separate stockpot, combine remaining ingredients except garnish; bring to a simmer. Add cooked tortellini; stir. Garnish with Parmesan cheese. Serves 3 to 4.

Dad's Tomato Comfort Soup

*Janeane O'Donnell
Omaha, NE*

When I was little, Dad made our lunch since Mom worked. We liked to try combining soups to create new flavors...this was one of our favorites!

14-1/2 oz. can diced tomatoes
10-3/4 oz. can tomato soup
14-1/2 oz. can beef broth

Optional: cooked rice or small
   soup pasta

In a stockpot over medium heat, combine undrained tomatoes and remaining ingredients. Simmer until heated through. Serves 2.

A fun new way to serve cornbread...waffle wedges or strips! Mix up the batter, thin it slightly with a little extra milk, then bake in a waffle iron until crisp. Terrific for dunking in soup or chili!

ABC Chicken Soup

Juana Rodriguez
American Falls, ID

Kids and grownups will enjoy eating this fun and hearty soup
on a cold winter day. We like it with warm corn tortillas.

2 T. oil
7-oz. pkg. alphabet pasta,
  uncooked
1/2 c. onion, minced
2 cubes tomato-chicken bouillon
3 roma tomatoes, chopped
6 c. water, divided

1 t. salt
2 c. deli rotisserie chicken
  breast, diced
Garnish: crumbled queso fresco
  or shredded Monterey Jack
  cheese, sliced avocado

Heat oil in a large saucepan over medium heat; add uncooked pasta.
Cook and stir until pasta is golden, about 3 to 4 minutes. Stir in onion
and bouillon cubes; cook until onion is soft. Remove saucepan from
heat. In a blender, blend tomatoes with 2 cups water. Add to saucepan
and return to heat. Add remaining water and salt; bring to a boil.
Cover and simmer for 7 minutes. Stir in chicken. Cover and simmer
for 7 additional minutes. Serve portions topped with cheese and
avocado slices. Makes 8 servings.

A toasty touch for soups! Butter bread slices and cut into shapes using
mini cookie cutters. Heat on a baking sheet at 425 degrees until crisp.
Place atop filled soup bowls at serving time.

Big Bend Clam Chowder

Mary Smith
Jacksonville, FL

This recipe was shared with me by my late Aunt Jo...it brings back so many wonderful memories! I loved to watch as she cut up the potatoes and onion. She always used home-canned tomatoes and fresh clams from Apalachicola, but it's good with canned clams too.

4 c. potatoes, peeled and finely
    diced
1 c. onion, finely diced
2-1/2 c. water
3/4 c. salt pork, finely diced

1/4 t. seasoned salt
3 c. tomatoes, finely diced
salt and pepper to taste
3 8-oz. cans minced clams,
    drained

Combine potatoes, onion and water in a large, heavy saucepan over medium heat. Meanwhile, in a skillet over medium-low heat, cook salt pork until drippings have cooked out, being careful not to burn. Add salt pork, drippings and seasoned salt to potato mixture. Simmer until vegetables are tender. Stir in tomatoes; cook 3 to 5 minutes. Add salt and pepper, as desired. Add clams and simmer until heated through; do not boil. Serves 6 to 8.

Oyster Cracker Magic

Joyce Hankey
Portland, OR

These crunchy morsels are tasty with soup or just for snacking.

12-oz. pkg. oyster crackers
1 T. dried, minced onion
1 T. dried parsley

1 t. dill weed
1 t. garlic powder
1 c. oil

Place crackers on an ungreased baking sheet. Mix remaining ingredients except oil together; sprinkle over crackers. Drizzle oil on top. Bake, uncovered, at 225 degrees for 20 minutes. Cool; store in an airtight container. Makes about 20 servings.

Soups, Breads & Sandwiches

Southern Corn Chowder

JoAlice Welton
Lawrenceville, GA

This recipe came from my mom, who taught Home Ec for many years before I was born. She was a fabulous Southern cook!

6 slices bacon, finely diced
1 stalk celery, thinly sliced
1 onion, diced
1 redskin potato, diced
1/4 c. all-purpose flour
1 T. butter
2 c. whole milk
1-1/2 c. chicken broth

2 c. frozen corn
3/4 t. salt
1/2 t. pepper
1/2 t. dried sage
1/2 t. dried thyme
1/4 t. celery salt
1/4 t. nutmeg
1/8 t. cayenne pepper

Sauté bacon in a Dutch oven or stockpot over medium heat. Add celery, onion and potato. Cook until potato starts to turn golden, about 5 to 7 minutes; drain. Stir in flour and butter. Cook just until mixture starts to bubble, about 3 to 5 minutes. Add remaining ingredients and bring to a boil. Reduce heat and cover. Simmer for 20 to 30 minutes, stirring 2 to 3 times, until potato is tender and chowder has thickened. Makes 4 to 6 servings.

For recipes that you make often, mix up several small bags
of the seasonings it calls for. Label with the recipe's name and
tuck in the cupboard...a terrific time-saver for future meals!

Country Skillet Soup

Pam Massey
Marshall, AR

I just love soup! My mother always made this hearty soup in the fall when the weather began to change. This recipe makes plenty of leftovers for lunch the next day, when it tastes even better...yum!

4 potatoes, peeled and cubed
1/2 onion, diced
2 c. water
3/4 c. frozen mixed vegetables

1/4 to 1/2 lb. ground beef
1 c. frozen corn
14-1/2 oz. can diced tomatoes
salt and pepper to taste

In a saucepan over medium-high heat, combine potatoes, onion and water. Bring to a boil; reduce heat and simmer until tender, about 10 minutes. Stir in mixed vegetables; remove from heat. Meanwhile, in a large, deep skillet over medium heat, brown beef; drain. Add corn to beef and cook until softened, about 2 minutes. Stir tomatoes into beef mixture; cook until tomatoes begin to soften, about 2 minutes. Carefully stir in potato mixture, adding liquid slowly; add salt and pepper to taste. Simmer for 20 minutes. Serves 6 to 8.

Miss Sheryl's Cornbread Muffins

Kristina Solid
Fayetteville, TN

Cornbread muffins aren't hard to make from scratch. This tasty recipe was given to me by a dear friend. My children ask for them for dinner all the time!

1 c. cornmeal
1 c. all-purpose flour
1/2 c. sugar
2-1/2 t. baking powder

1/4 t. salt
1 c. buttermilk
1/2 c. butter, softened
1 egg, beaten

Mix dry ingredients in a large bowl; set aside. Combine remaining ingredients in a separate bowl; add to dry ingredients. Stir until moistened. Divide batter evenly into 12 lightly greased muffin cups. Bake at 400 degrees for 15 to 20 minutes. Makes one dozen.

Haegen's Beef Stew

Krys Lewis
Vancouver, WA

*This hearty, filling recipe was handed down from my grandma.
The first time my children tried it, my oldest son liked it so much
that he named it after himself!*

1 lb. ground beef	1 cube beef bouillon
5 potatoes, peeled and cubed	1 T. onion powder
4 c. water	1/8 t. salt
15-oz. can peas, drained and liquid reserved	1/2 c. all-purpose flour

Brown beef in a stockpot over medium heat; drain. Add potatoes,
water, reserved liquid from peas, bouillon, onion powder and salt.
Simmer until potatoes are soft, about 30 minutes. Stir in flour; if
needed, add a little more water to make a light gravy. After gravy has
simmered for a few minutes, gently stir in peas. Let simmer for a few
minutes before serving. Serves 4 to 6.

Biscuit toppers make a hearty meal of a bowl of thick soup or stew.
Flatten jumbo refrigerated biscuits and arrange on an ungreased baking
sheet. Pierce several times with a fork and bake as package directs.
Place each topper on a bowl of hot, bubbly soup and serve.

Mushroom-Barley Beef Soup

Holly Vidourek
Cincinnati, OH

Rich and hearty...a meal in itself!

1/2 lb. stew beef, cubed
1 onion, chopped
8-oz. pkg. sliced mushrooms
1 T. olive oil

4 14-1/2 oz. cans beef broth
3/4 c. quick-cooking pearled
   barley, uncooked

Combine beef, onion, mushrooms and oil in a large saucepan. Cook over medium-high heat for about 10 minutes, or until beef is browned. Stir in broth; bring to a boil. Add barley. Reduce heat and simmer, covered, for 30 to 45 minutes, until beef and barley are tender. Makes 4 to 6 servings.

Adapt a family favorite soup, stew or chili to make in a slow cooker. A recipe that simmers for 2 hours on the stovetop can usually cook all day on the low setting without overcooking.

Creamy Wild Rice Soup

Brooke Sottosanti
Brunswick, OH

My kids love this soup...they're happy to eat it any time of the year!
I'm happy because it's easy to make. This is a delicious way to
use up the rice left over from last night's dinner too.

6-oz. pkg. long grain and wild
   rice mix, uncooked
1 lb. ground beef
14-1/2 oz. can chicken broth
10-3/4 oz. can cream of
   mushroom soup
2 c. milk

1 c. shredded Cheddar cheese
1/3 c. carrot, peeled and
   shredded
1-oz. pkg. ranch salad dressing
   mix
Garnish: chopped green onions

Prepare rice mix as package directs. Measure out 1-1/2 cups cooked rice and set aside, reserving the remainder for another use. Meanwhile, in a Dutch oven over medium heat, brown beef. Drain; stir in cooked rice and remaining ingredients except garnish. Reduce heat to low and simmer for 15 to 20 minutes, stirring often. Sprinkle servings with green onions. Serves 6 to 8.

Empty jars make handy vases when your child brings you a
hand-picked bouquet. Use them, too, when you take flowers to
a new mom or a homebound friend...there's no need for
the "vase" to be returned to you. Tie a raffia bow around
the jar for a sweet touch.

Pasta e Fagiole

Linda Romano
Canonsburg, PA

My grandmother and mother used to make this recipe. The name means Pasta and Beans...it's a traditional Italian peasant dish that's a great comfort on a cold, rainy day. The cannellini beans will give you a boost of energy!

8-oz. can tomato sauce
16-oz. can cannellini beans
dried parsley, salt and pepper
   to taste
Optional: 1 to 2 t. garlic powder

16-oz. can chicken broth
1 c. ditalini pasta, uncooked
Garnish: grated Parmesan or
   Romano cheese

In a saucepan over medium heat, combine tomato sauce, undrained beans and seasonings as desired. Reduce heat to low; cover and simmer for about an hour. When soup is nearly done, add broth to a separate saucepan; bring to a boil over medium-high heat. Add pasta and boil for 9 to 11 minutes. When pasta is tender, do not drain; add to tomato sauce mixture and heat through. Garnish with grated cheese. Serves 4 to 6.

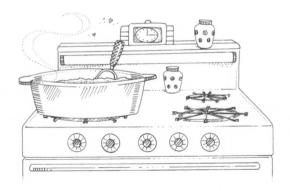

A squeaky-clean stovetop...no elbow grease required! Next time the soup boils over, cover cooked-on food spots with equal parts water and baking soda. Spills will soak right off.

Soups, Breads & *Sandwiches*

Lori's Rosemary Focaccia

Lori Peterson
Effingham, KS

I first tasted focaccia bread when I was a teen working at a local deli. Now I make it all the time. It's great by itself or made into a sandwich. Yummy, yummy!

3 c. bread flour
1 T. dried rosemary
1 T. sugar
1 t. salt
2-1/4 t. instant dry yeast

3 to 4 T. olive oil, divided
1 c. very warm water, 120 to 130 degrees
Optional: 1 c. shredded Cheddar cheese

In the order listed, place all ingredients except one tablespoon oil and Cheddar cheese into a bread machine. Set machine to dough cycle. When finished, divide dough in half. Form each half into a flattened 10-inch circle. Cover loosely with plastic wrap sprayed with non-stick vegetable spray. Let rise until double in size, about 30 minutes. Place on greased baking sheets. Brush tops with remaining oil; sprinkle with cheese, if desired. Bake at 400 degrees for 15 to 20 minutes, until golden. Makes 2 loaves.

Mommy's Pastrami on Focaccia

Regina Vining
Warwick, RI

I use toothpicks with little Italian flags on them to hold the sandwiches...and to make my kids giggle!

1 loaf focaccia bread, halved lengthwise
1/4 c. basil pesto
1/2 lb. deli pastrami, sliced
1/4 lb. deli ham, sliced

5 slices Provolone cheese
1/3 c. onion, thinly sliced
1 tomato, sliced
1/4 t. Italian seasoning

Spread cut sides of loaf with pesto. On bottom of loaf, layer meats, cheese, onion and tomato; sprinkle with seasoning. Add top of loaf. Wrap in aluminum foil; place on a baking sheet. Bake at 350 degrees for about 20 minutes, or until heated through. Let stand several minutes; cut into wedges. Makes 8 servings.

Yummy Italian Sausage Sandwiches
Irene Putman
Canal Fulton, OH

I can't even remember how long we've been making these sandwiches but they are a favorite of my children...and those kids are grown-ups! Now they are making sausage sandwiches for their own children. Try them, you'll love them too!

15-oz. can tomato sauce
1/2 t. dried basil
1/4 t. red pepper flakes
1/4 t. garlic powder
1 lb. Italian ground pork
   sausage, divided into
   4 flat patties

1 loaf Italian bread, sliced
   diagonally into 8 slices
4 slices mozzarella cheese
2 to 4 T. butter, softened

In a small saucepan over low heat, stir together tomato sauce and seasonings. Simmer until sauce thickens, about 8 to 10 minutes. Meanwhile, in a skillet over medium heat, cook sausage patties until browned and cooked through; drain. Top each of 4 bread slices with a warm patty, a slice of cheese and another slice of bread. Spread butter over the outside top and bottom slices of each sandwich. Grill sandwiches on a griddle over medium-high heat, turning once, until golden and cheese is melted. Ladle sauce into bowls and serve with sandwiches as a dipping sauce. Serves 4.

Cloth napkins are so much nicer than paper ones...why not whip up some fun napkin rings for them? Stitch a big vintage button or a pretty silk flower onto colorful new hair elastics...done in a snap!

Open-Faced Ham Bagels

Wendy Reaume
Ontario, Canada

Often I'm privileged to bring my seven-year-old daughter, Morgan, to work with me. This is one of our favorite lunchtime sandwiches! She can help me make them in the middle of a hectic morning. They're so tasty that my co-workers line up for the extras! Serve by themselves or alongside your favorite soup.

1 c. mayonnaise
1 c. deli ham, chopped
1 c. shredded Cheddar cheese
1 green onion, finely chopped

Optional: 1/2 c. bacon, crisply
   cooked and crumbled
3 to 4 bagels, halved

In a bowl, mix together all ingredients except bagels. Spread mixture onto the cut sides of bagel halves. Arrange bagels on a broiler pan. Broil for 5 minutes, until cheese is melted and bubbly. Serves 3 to 4.

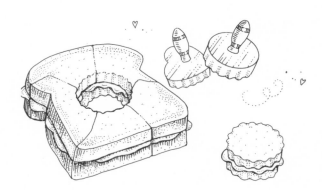

Delight finicky eaters with jigsaw puzzle sandwiches. Press a cookie cutter straight down in the center of a sandwich, then slice the outer part of sandwich into several pieces. It works great with grilled cheese or even peanut butter & jelly!

Stuffed French Rolls

Pam Schlimmer
San Jose, CA

This recipe from my childhood still brings back such special family memories. They're so easy to make too. Yum!

2 onions, chopped
1 T. oil
1-1/2 lbs. ground beef
8-oz. can tomato paste
4-oz. jar chopped pimentos, drained

2 2-1/4 oz. cans chopped black olives, drained
2 c. shredded Cheddar cheese
12 French rolls, centers hollowed out

In a skillet over medium heat, cook onion in oil until translucent, about 4 minutes. Add beef and cook an additional 5 minutes until browned; drain. Stir in remaining ingredients except rolls. Reduce heat to low and stir until cheese begins to melt, about 3 minutes. Stuff into hollowed-out rolls; serve immediately. Makes 12 servings.

Super Burgers

Diane Douglass
Tullahoma, TN

I've made family cookbooks for my kids...this recipe is one they've always asked for.

1 lb. ground beef
10-3/4 oz. can minestrone soup

8 hamburger buns, split
8 slices American cheese

Brown beef in a skillet over medium heat; drain. Add soup; mix well and heat through. Place bottoms of buns on an ungreased baking sheet. Divide beef mixture evenly over bottoms of buns. Top each with a cheese slice. Broil just until bubbly, about 2 to 3 minutes. Replace tops and serve. Makes 8 servings.

Pulled Turkey Barbecue

Mildred Gochenour
Harrisonburg, VA

I found this recipe because one of my daughters doesn't eat red meat. Now she requests it whenever she comes to visit! If time is short, just simmer the turkey and sauce on the stovetop for 30 minutes to one hour instead of slow-cooking it.

2-1/2 to 3 lbs. boneless turkey
   tenderloins, cubed
3/4 c. catsup
1/2 c. vinegar
1/2 c. Worcestershire sauce
1/2 c. oil
4 t. lemon juice

3/4 c. brown sugar, packed
4 t. salt
4 t. dry mustard
4 t. chili powder
4 t. paprika
2 t. cayenne pepper
12 hamburger buns, split

Place turkey in a stockpot with enough water to cover it. Place lid on pot; bring to a boil over medium-high heat. Reduce heat and simmer until turkey is very tender; drain well. Use 2 forks to shred turkey; add to a slow cooker and set aside. In a bowl, combine catsup, vinegar, Worcestershire sauce, oil and lemon juice. Mix well; stir in remaining ingredients except buns. Add catsup mixture to turkey as desired. Cover and cook on low setting for 2 to 3 hours. Serve on buns. Makes 12 servings.

Mix up some fresh coleslaw in a jiffy...combine a package of pre-shredded coleslaw mix and bottled coleslaw dressing to taste. Stir in a drained can of mandarin oranges for a sweet twist. Perfect with barbecue!

Brilliant Brick Sandwiches

Linda Kilgore
Kittanning, PA

This is my husband's recipe. One day he told the kids and me that he was making "brick sandwiches" for supper. The three of us just thought, OK, this better be good! Well...I believe it was the best sandwich I ever ate. The brick flattens the sandwich and cooks all the ingredients together. Absolutely delicious!

12 thick slices Italian bread
1 lb. deli baked ham, thinly
    sliced
1 lb. Swiss cheese, thinly sliced
1 onion, thinly sliced

1 tomato, thinly sliced
1/2 to 1 c. shredded lettuce
2 to 3 T. mayonnaise
1 T. olive oil

Wrap a clean new brick in aluminum foil. Place brick on an electric griddle; preheat over medium-high heat. Layer 6 bread slices with remaining ingredients except mayonnaise and oil. Spread one side of remaining bread slices with mayonnaise; close sandwiches. Brush outsides of sandwiches with oil. Place one sandwich on hot griddle; set the brick on top of the sandwich. Cook until sandwich is golden on both sides. Repeat with remaining sandwiches. Serves 6.

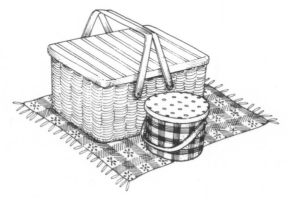

Wicker picnic baskets just like Mom's are easy to find at
tag sales...they bring back fond childhood memories of picnic
fun! When yours isn't being used to tote picnic goodies, keep it
in the kitchen to hold a collection of favorite cookbooks.

Soups, Breads & *Sandwiches*

Daddy's Potato Sandwiches

Lorrie Smith
Drummonds, TN

My dad made these for me when I was a little girl. He didn't do much cooking, so they were always a special treat. When I became a teenager, I started making them myself as an after-school snack. I still love them now, years later. Serve with large glasses of iced tea.

1 to 2 t. oil
1 potato, peeled and sliced into
   thin rounds

Optional: 1/2 onion, sliced
4 slices white bread
salt and catsup to taste

Heat oil in a cast-iron skillet over medium heat. Add potato slices; cook until tender and golden on both sides. Remove to a paper towel-covered plate. Sauté onion until translucent, if using; remove to plate. Layer potatoes and onion on 2 bread slices. Add salt and catsup; top with remaining bread slices. Serves 2.

Homemade Spicy Catsup

Gail Prather
Hastings, NE

Deliciously fresh and different! Over the years, I've blended a couple of different recipes together to create this one.

3 6-oz. cans tomato paste
3/4 c. cider vinegar
1/4 c. brown sugar, packed
1/4 c. honey
1 t. salt
1/2 t. cinnamon

1/4 t. ground cloves
1/8 t. cayenne pepper
1/8 t. allspice
1/8 t. garlic powder
1/4 to 1/2 c. water

In a saucepan over medium-low heat, combine all ingredients except water. Stir in water to desired consistency; bring to a boil. Reduce heat to low; simmer, uncovered, for 5 minutes, stirring occasionally. Cool. Pour into a glass jar; cover and refrigerate. Makes 2 to 2-1/2 cups.

Midway Corn Dogs

Jane Davis
Bluffton, OH

My mom shared this yummy corn dog recipe with me. Not only are they great when just cooked...you can keep them in the fridge overnight and they are wonderful warmed up in the microwave!

16-oz. pkg. hot dogs
1 c. yellow cornmeal
1 c. all-purpose flour
1/2 c. sugar
4 t. baking powder

2 t. salt
1 egg, beaten
1 c. milk
oil for deep frying
Garnish: mustard, catsup

Pat hot dogs dry with a paper towel; set aside. In a bowl, stir together cornmeal, flour, sugar, baking powder and salt. Add egg and milk; beat until smooth. In a deep saucepan, heat several inches of oil to 375 degrees. Dip hot dogs in batter and add to oil, several at a time. Keep turning hot dogs until golden on all sides. Place on paper towels to drain. Serve with mustard and catsup. Makes 8 to 10 servings.

Whip up some soda shoppe treats at your next get-together...enjoy a pink or brown cow! Add a big scoop of vanilla ice cream to a tall glass, then top off with fizzy red pop or root beer.

Fried Jam Sandwich

Debra Suits
Albany, NY

My mom made these tasty sandwiches when we were growing up.
During the winter months, we often enjoyed them with hot cocoa
after a sleigh ride. Not exactly a diet recipe...but it is delicious!

1 egg, beaten
1 T. milk
1/2 t. cinnamon
1 t. sugar

2 slices white bread
2 t. favorite-flavor jam or jelly
2 t. butter

Whisk together egg, milk, cinnamon and sugar in a bowl. Make a
sandwich with bread slices and jam or jelly; dip both sides into egg
mixture. In a skillet over medium heat, fry in butter until golden on
both sides. Serves one.

Blueberry Freezer Jam

Mary Lou Thomas
Portland, ME

One sweet taste brings back special memories of summer
berry-picking with my mother and sisters.

6 c. blueberries, crushed
5 c. sugar
2 T. lemon juice
3/4 c. water

1-3/4 oz. pkg. powdered pectin
7 1/2-pint freezer-safe plastic
    containers and lids,
    sterilized

Combine berries, sugar and lemon juice in a bowl; let stand for
10 minutes. In a small saucepan over medium-high heat, bring water
and pectin to a boil. Cook and stir for one minute. Add to berry
mixture; stir for 3 minutes. Ladle into freezer containers; cool to room
temperature. Cover and let stand overnight at room temperature
before freezing. May be frozen up to one year. Keep refrigerated up
to 3 weeks after opening. Makes 7 containers.

Hearty Wheat Bread

Melanie Lowe
Dover, DE

When I smell this bread baking, I'm reminded of winter afternoons
as a little girl, when my mother taught me how to bake.

1-1/2 c. warm water, 110 to
   115 degrees
1/3 c. plus 1 T. brown sugar,
   packed and divided
2 envs. active dry yeast

2 c. all-purpose flour, divided
4 c. whole-wheat flour, divided
2 t. salt
1/3 c. oil
1/2 c. milk, room temperature

Pour warm water into a large bowl; stir in one tablespoon brown
sugar. Sprinkle yeast on water; let stand for 10 minutes. Add one cup
all-purpose flour, 3 cups whole-wheat flour, salt, oil and milk to yeast
mixture. Beat with an electric mixer on medium speed. Gradually add
remaining flour, 1/2 cup at a time; beat for about 5 minutes. Place
dough in a greased bowl; turn to coat and cover loosely. Let rise for
about one hour, until double in size. Punch down; divide into 2 equal
balls. On a floured surface, roll each ball into a 16-inch by 8-inch
rectangle. Roll up into loaves; pinch seams together. Put loaves
seam-side down into 2 greased 9"x5" loaf pans. Make several slashes
across tops with a serrated knife. Let rise again until double in size,
about 30 to 45 minutes. Bake at 400 degrees for 15 minutes. Reduce
oven to 350 degrees; bake an additional 30 minutes, or until golden.
Remove to wire racks to cool. Makes 2 loaves.

Thrift shops always have heaps of gently used baskets.
Keep several on hand and you'll be ready to put together a gift
at a moment's notice. Tuck in a jar of jam and a loaf of
fresh-baked bread wrapped up in a tea towel...so thoughtful!

Homestyle French Bread

Denise Webb
Galveston, IN

*I've been making this wonderful bread for over thirty years. It is
easy to make, delicious and with two loaves, there's always
one to enjoy and one to share...so neighborly!*

2 envs. active dry yeast	3 T. sugar
1/2 c. warm water, 110 to	1 T. salt
115 degrees	1/3 c. oil
2 c. hot water, 120 to	6 c. all-purpose flour, divided
130 degrees	1 egg white, beaten

In a cup, dissolve yeast in 1/2 cup warm water; set aside. In a large
bowl, combine hot water, sugar, salt, oil and 3 cups flour; stir well.
Stir in yeast mixture. Add remaining flour and stir well with a heavy
spoon. Leave spoon in the dough; allow dough to rest 10 minutes.
Stir; let dough rest another 10 minutes. Repeat this process 3 more
times, making 5 times in all. Turn dough onto a lightly floured board.
Knead just enough to coat dough with flour; divide it into 2 equal
balls. Roll out each ball into a 12-inch by 9-inch rectangle; roll up
lengthwise, pinching together seams. Place loaves seam-side down
on a greased baking sheet, allowing room for both to rise. Cover; let
rise in a warm place for 30 minutes. With a very sharp knife, cut
3 diagonal slashes in the top of each loaf; brush with egg white. Bake
at 400 degrees for about 30 minutes, or until crusty and golden.
Remove to wire racks to cool. Makes 2 loaves.

Tea towels from the 1950s
are perfect bread-basket
liners...they'll keep freshly
baked bread toasty warm
and add a dash of color
to the table.

Pillow-Soft Dinner Rolls

Debi DeVore
New Philadelphia, OH

Homemade rolls that deserve the freshest dairy butter...yum!

4-1/2 t. active dry yeast
1/2 c. warm water, 110 to
   115 degrees
2 c. warm milk, 110 to
   115 degrees
6 T. shortening

2 eggs, beaten
1/4 c. sugar
1-1/2 t. salt
7 to 7-1/2 c. all-purpose flour,
   divided

In a large bowl, dissolve yeast in warm water. Add warm milk, shortening, eggs, sugar, salt and 3 cups flour. Beat until smooth. Stir in enough of remaining flour to form a soft dough. Turn onto a floured surface; knead until smooth and elastic, 6 to 8 minutes. Dough will be sticky. Place in a greased bowl; turn once to grease top. Cover; let rise in a warm place until double in size, about one hour. Punch down dough; turn onto a lightly floured surface. Divide into 24 pieces; form each into a roll. Arrange on greased baking sheets, 2 inches apart. Cover and let rise until double in size, about 30 minutes. Bake at 350 degrees for 20 to 25 minutes, until golden. Remove to wire racks to cool. Makes 2 dozen.

Dress up homemade bread or dinner rolls...it's easy. Before baking, brush the dough with a little beaten egg, then sprinkle with sesame seed, grated Parmesan or dried rosemary.

Italian Yeast Rolls

Tina George
El Dorado, AR

These herbed rolls will make any spaghetti dinner memorable!

1-1/2 c. warm water, 110 to
   115 degrees
2 T. oil
1 t. lemon juice
2 t. salt
3 T. sugar

2 T. powdered milk
4 c. all-purpose flour
1 T. Italian seasoning
1 T. garlic powder
1-1/2 t. instant dry yeast
3 T. butter, melted

In the order listed, add all ingredients except butter into a bread machine. Set machine to dough cycle. Allow to process for 1-1/2 to 2 hours; do not open the lid. When finished, roll dough into twelve, 2-inch balls. Place on a baking sheet sprayed with non-stick vegetable spray. Brush tops of rolls with butter. Bake at 350 degrees for about 15 minutes, or until golden. Makes one dozen.

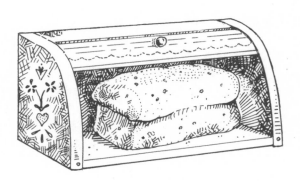

Want to try making your favorite conventional bread recipe using a bread machine? It's simple. If the recipe makes 2 loaves, just divide all the ingredients in half to produce one bread-machine loaf. Don't divide the amount of yeast, though...it should still be about 2 teaspoons.

Apple-Cheese Biscuits

Jerri Duncan-Shay
Stewartsville, MO

*My mother always made these on Christmas morning...we couldn't
wait to dig in! Mom is no longer with us, but each time I
make them, I think of her.*

1/3 c. sugar
1/3 c. sweetened flaked coconut
1/2 t. cinnamon
3 T. margarine, melted
1-3/4 c. biscuit baking mix

3/4 c. shredded Cheddar cheese
1 tart apple, cored, peeled
and diced
1/3 c. plus 1 T. milk

Stir together sugar, coconut and cinnamon in a cup. Place margarine
in another cup; set aside. In a medium bowl, stir together biscuit mix,
cheese and apple; make a well in the center. Add milk all at once,
stirring just until dough holds together. Form dough into 16 balls. Dip
in margarine; roll in sugar mixture. Arrange in a greased 9" round
baking pan. Bake at 400 degrees for about 25 minutes. Makes 16.

Mini Cheddar Loaves

Mary King
Ashville, AL

*Mother and I have enjoyed this simple recipe for many
years...it's great to take to parties and potlucks.*

2-1/2 c. shredded Cheddar
cheese
3-1/2 c. biscuit baking mix

2 eggs, beaten
1-1/4 c. milk

Combine cheese and biscuit mix in a large bowl. In a separate bowl,
beat together eggs and milk; stir into cheese mixture. Pour into
2 greased 7"x4" loaf pans. Bake at 350 degrees for 40 to 55 minutes.
Check for doneness after 40 minutes by inserting a toothpick near
center. If not done, bake an additional 5 minutes and test again.
Repeat until done. Makes 2 mini loaves.

Sides
&Salads

Homestyle Shells & Cheese

Kathy Mason
LaPorte, IN

When I ask my son what we should have for any upcoming holiday dinner, this scrumptious dish is always his first response!

16-oz. pkg. medium shell
  macaroni, uncooked
16-oz. container sour cream
16-oz. container cottage cheese
1 bunch green onions, minced
1 egg, beaten
2 c. shredded Colby Jack cheese

2 c. shredded sharp Cheddar
  cheese
salt and pepper to taste
1/2 c. butter, melted and divided
1 c. Italian-flavored dry bread
  crumbs

Cook macaroni according to package directions; drain and set aside. Meanwhile, in a bowl, mix together sour cream, cottage cheese, onions and egg. Stir in cheeses, salt and pepper; add cooked macaroni and mix well. Coat a 13"x9" baking pan with 2 tablespoons melted butter. Spread mixture evenly in pan. Toss remaining butter with bread crumbs and sprinkle over top. Bake, uncovered, at 350 degrees for 30 to 40 minutes, until cheese is bubbly and bread crumbs are golden. Makes 10 to 12 servings.

Shake up family favorite noodle dishes by using different styles of pasta. Add interest with curly corkscrews, cavatelli shells or wagon wheels...even spinach-flavored or rainbow pasta.

Cheesy Scalloped Potatoes

Debbie Osborn
Westerville, OH

My mother served these potatoes every year for our Easter dinner.
They're delicious alongside a baked ham.

1/4 c. butter
1/4 c. all-purpose flour
2 c. milk
8-oz. pkg. shredded sharp
   Cheddar cheese

1 t. salt
1/4 t. pepper
5 potatoes, peeled and sliced
2 onions, sliced

Melt butter in a saucepan over low heat; blend in flour and cook for
one minute. Whisk in milk. Cook, stirring constantly, until slightly
thickened. Stir in cheese until melted. Add salt and pepper. Spread half
of sauce in the bottom of a greased 13"x9" glass baking pan. Arrange
potatoes and onions over sauce; top with remaining sauce. Bake,
uncovered, at 350 degrees for about one hour, until potatoes are
tender. Makes 8 servings.

Crunchy Hasselback Potatoes

Heidi Fontes
Brighton, CO

Guests will love these savory baked potatoes, and the fanned-out
slices are so pretty on the dinner plate.

8 baking potatoes
3 T. olive oil, divided
1/4 c. grated Parmesan cheese
1/2 c. soft bread crumbs

1 t. garlic salt
salt to taste
Garnish: sour cream, shredded
   Cheddar cheese, bacon bits

With a sharp knife, slice each potato several times from side to side,
about 1/4-inch apart, not quite through to the bottom. Place potatoes
on a lightly greased baking sheet. Brush potatoes with 2 tablespoons
oil. Mix together remaining oil and other ingredients except garnish.
Spoon mixture evenly over potatoes; gently pat mixture between
potato slices. Cover with aluminum foil. Bake at 400 degrees for
35 minutes. Uncover; bake an additional 20 minutes. Add toppings
as desired. Makes 8 servings.

Citrus-Mint Orzo Salad

JoAlice Welton
Lawrenceville, GA

*This recipe is a family favorite from my late mom. It is
a much-requested dish for gatherings with family & friends.*

16-oz. pkg. orzo pasta,
   uncooked
1 c. olive oil & vinegar salad
   dressing
1/2 c. frozen orange juice
   concentrate, thawed
1/2 c. fresh mint, minced
1/2 c. dried apricots, chopped
1 c. currants

1 c. slivered almonds, toasted
1 c. sun-dried tomatoes,
   chopped
1 green pepper, diced
1 c. red onion, minced
Optional: 1 c. goat cheese, cubed
salt and pepper to taste
Garnish: thin orange slices,
   fresh mint sprigs

Cook orzo according to package directions; drain and rinse with cold
water. Measure out 3 cups cooked orzo into a large serving bowl;
reserve remaining orzo for another recipe. In a separate bowl, whisk
together salad dressing, orange juice and mint. Drizzle dressing over
orzo and mix well. Add remaining ingredients except garnish; toss
gently. Garnish as desired. Serves 6 to 8.

Bring out Mom's old printed tablecloths and use them...they're too
much fun to hide away! Red strawberries, cowboys & cowgirls,
vacation spots and other whimsical designs will delight your kids and
bring back fond memories of family meals years ago.

Mediterranean Couscous Salad

Kathy White
Cato, NY

This is a new recipe for our family and it's a real keeper! The light, fresh taste makes it a great main dish or an excellent side, whether it's served hot or chilled.

10-oz. pkg. couscous, uncooked
1/4 c. plus 1 T. olive oil, divided
1/2 c. lemon juice
1 t. Italian seasoning
15-1/2 oz. can black beans,
   drained and rinsed

6-oz. pkg. baby spinach
1 t. salt
1/2 t. pepper

Prepare couscous according to package directions; drain and set aside. In a saucepan over medium heat, combine 1/4 cup oil, lemon juice and Italian seasoning. Bring to a low boil; stir in beans and cook until warmed through. Meanwhile, add remaining oil to a skillet over medium heat; add spinach and cook until wilted. Add bean mixture to spinach and stir gently. Stir in couscous, salt and pepper. Serve immediately, or chill overnight and serve cold. Makes 8 to 10 servings.

Encourage kids to eat all kinds of veggies! Cut up fresh veggies into easy-to-handle pieces. Serve with small cups of creamy peanut butter, ranch salad dressing, hummus or salsa for dipping...yummy!

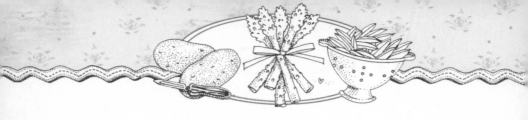

Golden Crumb Broccoli Casserole

Pam Glover
Castle Rock, CO

I've been making this saucy broccoli dish for special occasions for about twenty years now and it's still a favorite! Even people who are not crazy about broccoli (like my husband!) enjoy it. If you like, use 6 cups steamed fresh broccoli instead of frozen broccoli.

10-3/4 oz. can cream of
   mushroom soup
1/4 c. mayonnaise
1/2 c. shredded Cheddar cheese

1-1/2 t. lemon juice
3 10-oz. pkgs. frozen broccoli,
   cooked and drained
1/2 c. cheese crackers, crushed

In a large bowl, combine soup, mayonnaise, cheese and lemon juice. Add broccoli and toss to combine well. Transfer mixture to a greased shallow 1-1/2 quart casserole dish. Top with crackers. Bake, uncovered, at 350 degrees for 35 minutes, until hot and bubbly. Serves 6 to 8.

Vintage magazine recipe ads make fun wall art for the kitchen.
They're easy to find at flea markets...look for ones featuring
shimmery gelatin salads, golden macaroni & cheese or
other favorites like Mom used to make!

Tina's Herbed Corn

Tina George
El Dorado, AR

*I serve this side dish with everything from spaghetti to roast chicken
to barbecue...my family loves it! It's also a quick & easy dish
to carry to a potluck.*

6 c. frozen corn	1/2 t. dill weed
1/2 c. water	1/4 t. garlic powder
1/4 c. butter, sliced	1/4 t. Italian seasoning
1 T. dried parsley	1/8 t. dried thyme
1 t. salt	

In a large saucepan over medium-high heat, combine corn and water.
Bring to a boil. Reduce heat; cover and simmer for 4 to 6 minutes,
until corn is tender. Drain. Stir in remaining ingredients and heat
through before serving. Serves 6 to 8.

Easy Baked Corn

Susan Maher
Arnold, MD

Yummy and easy! Garnish with a sprinkle of parsley or paprika.

2 c. frozen corn, thawed	3 T. sugar
2 eggs, beaten	2 T. all-purpose flour
1/4 c. butter, sliced	1/4 t. salt
3/4 c. milk	

Place all ingredients in a blender or food processor; process to a
slightly chunky consistency. Pour into a greased 2-quart casserole dish.
Bake, uncovered, at 375 degrees for 45 minutes. Makes 6 servings.

Small glass knobs and drawer pulls make useful tea-towel hangers in
the kitchen...just attach the screws to a peg board.

Sweet-and-Sour Green Beans

Sue Giljum
Saint Louis, MO

My mom's family served this dish quite often. Now my own children have been asking for it, so the tradition will live on. If you like sweet-and-sour dishes, this will be a new favorite.

6 slices bacon, crisply cooked
   and crumbled, 2 T. drippings
   reserved
2/3 c. white vinegar
1/3 c. water

2/3 c. sugar
2 14-1/2 oz. cans green beans,
   drained
1/2 onion, sliced

In a saucepan over medium heat, place reserved drippings, vinegar and water. Bring to a boil. Slowly add sugar, stirring until dissolved. Add green beans and stir. Place onion slices on top of beans. Let boil for about 2 minutes; remove from heat. Cover and refrigerate for about 2 hours, stirring occasionally. Add crumbled bacon at serving time. Makes 6 servings.

Add an extra can or two of soup, vegetables or tuna to the grocery cart every week, then put aside these extras at home. Before you know it, you'll have a generous selection of canned goods for the local food pantry. A terrific lesson for kids to share in!

Glorified Green Beans

Natasha Morris
Lamar, CO

Last year my mom's paternal family put together a family cookbook. It has many great and simple recipes in it. Some of our wonderful cooks have left us, but when we serve up their recipes it brings back many fond memories. This quick and pretty dish was shared by two of my great-aunts.

2 to 3 slices bacon, crisply
    cooked and crumbled,
    2 T. drippings reserved
1 onion, chopped
2 14-1/2 oz. cans green beans,
    drained

10-oz. can diced tomatoes with
    chiles
1 T. prepared horseradish

Add reserved drippings to a saucepan over medium-high heat. Sauté onion until translucent. Add green beans and tomatoes; heat through. Stir in horseradish and serve. Makes 8 to 10 servings.

Create a family art gallery. Spray-paint a bulletin board a bright color
and decorate the frame with textured paint. Glue buttons
or charms to thumbtacks with craft glue, then display your children's
drawings and paintings with pride.

Phyllis's Napa Salad

Brenda Huey
Geneva, IN

This crunchy salad is fantastic! My family loves it. My wonderful friend, Phyllis, gave me this recipe and now it's a must whenever we have Chinese take-out for dinner.

1 head napa cabbage, sliced
6 green onions, chopped
1/2 c. margarine
2 3-oz. pkgs. Oriental-flavored
   ramen noodles, crushed

1/2 c. sunflower kernels
1/4 c. slivered almonds

Place cabbage and onions in a plastic zipping bag; refrigerate for one hour. In a saucepan over medium-low heat, melt margarine and add crushed ramen noodles, contents of seasoning packets and remaining ingredients. Sauté until golden. Cool; drain on a paper towel. In a large bowl, combine cabbage mixture and noodle mixture. Pour Napa Dressing over all; toss to coat. Serves 10 to 12.

Napa Dressing:

1 c. oil
1 c. sugar

1/2 c. cider vinegar
2 T. soy sauce

Whisk ingredients together until well blended.

Need a quick, tasty side? Stir sautéed diced mushrooms, onion, green pepper or celery into prepared wild rice mix for a homemade touch.

7-Layer Chinese Chicken Salad

Ann Mathis
Biscoe, AR

This crunchy, flavorful salad is terrific for a light lunch or supper.

5 c. romaine lettuce, shredded
3-oz. pkg. Oriental-flavored
   ramen noodles
2 c. cooked chicken, finely
   chopped
11-oz. can shoepeg corn,
   drained

1 tomato, finely chopped
2 green onions, finely chopped
1/2 c. unsalted dry-roasted
   peanuts, coarsely chopped
1/4 c. sunflower kernels

Arrange lettuce in a clear glass serving bowl. Coarsely crush ramen noodles, reserving seasoning packet for another use. Layer noodles and remaining ingredients over lettuce in order listed. Drizzle salad with Ginger Dressing; serve immediately. Serves 6.

Ginger Dressing:

1/4 c. oil
3 T. cider vinegar
2 T. sugar

3/4 t. ground ginger
1 t. salt
1/2 t. pepper

Combine ingredients in a small jar with a tight-fitting lid. Shake until well blended.

Invite friends over for a salad supper on a steamy summer day. Ask everyone to bring along a favorite salad. You provide crispy bread sticks or a loaf of zucchini bread and a pitcher of iced tea...relax and enjoy!

Cheesy Chile Rice

Wendy Reaume
Ontario, Canada

When I was growing up, my mom made this simple rice dish whenever we had Mexican food for dinner. It's yummy with burritos and tortilla chips. To this day, when my parents visit from Missouri, one of the first meals my mom makes is Mexican food with cheesy rice. It just wouldn't be the same without it!

2 c. water
2 c. instant rice, uncooked
16-oz. container sour cream

4-oz. can diced green chiles
3 c. shredded Cheddar cheese, divided

In a saucepan over medium-high heat, bring water to a boil. Stir in rice; remove from heat. Cover and let stand 5 minutes, until water is absorbed. In a large bowl, mix together rice, sour cream, chiles and 2 cups cheese. Spread in a greased 2-quart casserole dish; top with remaining cheese. Bake, uncovered, at 400 degrees for 30 minutes, until cheese is melted and top is lightly golden. Makes 6 servings.

If you're putting together a family cookbook, be sure to ask your kids about their favorite foods. You may find you have traditions in your own family that you weren't even aware of!

Dirty Greek Rice

Bea Garcia
San Antonio, TX

This savory rice goes well with chicken, beef and fish...in other words, with just about anything! It's been a family favorite for twenty-five years.

4 slices bacon, crisply cooked and crumbled, drippings reserved
1-1/2 c. long-cooking rice, uncooked
6 green onions, chopped

2 cloves garlic, minced
2-1/4 oz. can sliced black olives, drained
1 t. Greek seasoning
1 t. salt
3 c. water

Heat reserved drippings in a skillet over medium heat. Add rice and sauté, cooking and stirring until golden. Add remaining ingredients including crumbled bacon. Bring to a boil; reduce heat to low. Cover and simmer for 35 to 40 minutes, until rice is tender. Fluff with a fork before serving. Serves 6.

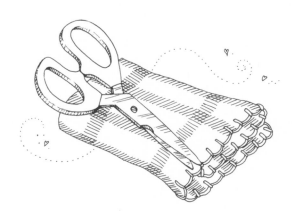

To chop green onions in a jiffy, use a pair of kitchen shears.

Special Peas & Carrots

Annette Mullan
North Arlington, NJ

I came up with this simple recipe when my children were younger and wouldn't eat their veggies...it really did the trick!

1-1/2 T. extra-virgin olive oil
1/4 onion, finely chopped
14-1/2 oz. can peas and carrots, drained

salt and pepper to taste

In a saucepan over medium heat, heat oil until hot but not smoking. Add onion and sauté until translucent. Add peas and carrots; stir gently. Sprinkle with salt and pepper; heat through. Serves 4.

Yummy Carrots

Tina Wright
Atlanta, GA

My kids sure love these carrots! My youngest son even suggested we leave them out for the Easter Bunny because they taste so good.

2 c. carrots, peeled and chopped
1 clove garlic, minced
1 t. dill weed

2 T. butter
salt and pepper to taste

Place carrots in a saucepan; add just enough water to cover. Bring to a boil over medium-high heat. Cook for 3 to 5 minutes, until tender; drain. Add remaining ingredients; reduce heat to medium. Sauté lightly until butter is melted and carrots are heated through. Makes 4 servings.

Spiff up pantry shelves with pretty paper borders just like Mom used to have. Cut colorful paper with decorative-edged scissors and attach to shelf edges with double-sided tape...done in no time!

Peas & Dumplings

Teresa Amert
Upper Sandusky, OH

We children always sat together and shelled the peas after Mama picked them from the garden. Who could find the most peas in one pod? That kept our interest and made shelling peas fun instead of a chore. Then straight into the boiling water went the young peas, while we waited with our mouths watering for this simple, melt-in-your-mouth dish.

2 c. fresh peas
1/2 c. butter
1/2 c. all-purpose flour

4 c. milk
salt and pepper to taste

In a stockpot over medium-high heat, place peas in enough water to cover. Boil until tender, about 3 to 4 minutes. Drain and set aside. In the same stockpot, melt butter over medium heat. Whisk in flour and stir until thickened, about one to 2 minutes. Gradually add milk, stirring constantly. Reduce heat to low and add peas, salt and pepper. Drop Dumplings by tablespoonfuls on top of peas. Cover and cook over low heat for 15 to 20 minutes, testing dumplings for doneness with a fork. Serves 6.

Dumplings:

2 c. all-purpose flour
1 T. baking powder
1 t. salt

1/4 c. shortening
1 c. milk

Combine flour, baking powder and salt; lightly blend in shortening. Add milk all at once and stir.

When hand-washing delicate heirloom china, lay a tea towel in the bottom of the sink. It will pad the sink and protect against chipping.

Bubble & Squeak

Andrea Ford
Montfort, WI

This was one of my mom's recipes. It's a traditional English dish...it's tasty too, so give it a try!

2 c. cabbage, finely shredded
1 onion, chopped
3 T. butter

salt and pepper to taste
2 c. mashed potatoes

Place cabbage in a stockpot; add a small amount of salted water. Cook over medium heat for 15 minutes; drain well and set aside. In a skillet, sauté onion in butter until tender. Add cabbage, salt and pepper. Cook over low heat for 2 minutes. Fold in mashed potatoes until well blended. Spoon mixture onto a hot, lightly greased griddle, leaving a 1/2-inch margin around edge of griddle. Cook for 20 minutes, turning once, until golden on both sides. Serves 6.

Red Cabbage & Apple

Peggy Frazier
Indianapolis, IN

My father used to fix this recipe and it is really yummy! I prefer crisper cabbage, but for softer old-fashioned cabbage, increase the cooking time to 25 to 30 minutes.

1 T. bacon drippings or oil
2 c. red cabbage, shredded
1 c. apple, cored and cubed
2 T. brown sugar, packed
2 T. white vinegar

2 T. water
1/4 t. caraway seed
1/2 t. salt
1/8 t. pepper

Heat drippings or oil in a skillet over medium heat. Add remaining ingredients; cover tightly. Cook over low heat for about 15 minutes, stirring occasionally, to desired tenderness. Makes 4 to 6 servings.

Sides & *Salads*

Scalloped Cabbage

Sara Brunsvold
Mission, KS

One of my all-time favorite dishes! This recipe was perfected by my grandmother, who got it from her own mother. Grandma's secret was fresh cream from our dairy farm.

1 c. butter, divided
1/2 head cabbage, torn into
    bite-size pieces
3 sleeves round, buttery
    crackers, divided

salt and pepper to taste
2-1/2 c. whipping cream or milk
1 egg, beaten

In a stockpot over medium heat, melt 1/4 cup butter. Add cabbage and cook until translucent, about 10 to 15 minutes. Grease a 2-quart casserole dish; add 2 sleeves crackers, finely crushed, to form a crust along the bottom and sides of dish. Layer cabbage over crackers; sprinkle with salt and pepper. Cube remaining butter and place evenly over cabbage. Top with remaining sleeve of crackers, coarsely crushed. Pour cream or milk evenly over casserole; slowly pour egg evenly over top layer. Bake, uncovered, at 350 degrees for 45 to 50 minutes, until liquid is absorbed and crust is golden. Makes 6 to 8 servings.

If your favorite casserole tends to drip or bubble over in the oven, place a sheet of aluminum foil under the pan to catch drippings...clean-up's a snap!

Old-Fashioned Potato Salad

Christina Mamula
Aliquippa, PA

This is the best potato salad ever. It is greatly requested at baby and bridal showers, reunions and picnics. My mom was as old-fashioned as they came...everything in this recipe was measured with the cap off the bottle and "about that much" in a coffee cup. One day, my sister-in-law and I measured everything and we've got it down now. Mom surely left us something special to hand down through generations.

7 lbs. potatoes, peeled and
    cubed
2-1/2 c. mayonnaise-style salad
    dressing
1 T. cider vinegar
2 T. mustard
2 t. dill pickle juice

3/4 c. sugar
1/3 c. milk
1 doz. eggs, hard-boiled, peeled,
    sliced and divided
4 stalks celery, chopped
1 onion, chopped

Place potatoes in a large stockpot; add enough water to cover. Boil over medium-high heat for 25 to 30 minutes, until potatoes are just tender enough to cut easily with the side of a fork. Drain potatoes but do not rinse; put in a large bowl and set aside to cool. In a separate bowl, combine salad dressing, vinegar, mustard, pickle juice, sugar and milk. Whisk together until smooth. Add boiled eggs to cooled potatoes, reserving 12 to 15 slices for garnish. Add celery and onion and mix. Pour dressing mixture over top and toss gently. Arrange reserved egg slices on top. Cover and refrigerate 3 to 4 hours before serving. Serves 12.

Hard-boiled eggs, easy! Cover eggs with an inch of water in a saucepan and place over medium-high heat. As soon as the water boils, cover the pan and remove from heat. Let stand for 18 to 20 minutes...cover with ice water, peel and they're done!

Country Pea & Bean Salad

Sandy Brummett
Henderson, TX

My husband loves this salad...there are lots of loving memories in it! It was served every Thanksgiving at my parents. Now I have the salad bowl that Mother used to fix it in and I still use it every Thanksgiving for this salad.

15-oz. can shoepeg corn, drained
15-1/4 oz. can peas, drained
14-1/2 oz. can French-style green beans, drained

2-oz. jar chopped pimentos, drained
1 green pepper, chopped
1 onion, chopped
3 stalks celery, chopped

Combine all ingredients in a large bowl; toss to mix. Cover and chill overnight before serving. Serves 12.

Enamelware dishpans are so useful in the kitchen...don't pass them by at tag sales! They're perfect for mixing up company-size batches of salad, dressing and so much more...even for serving popcorn on family movie night!

Creamed Cucumbers

Diane Nichols
Wiota, IA

This tasty recipe is from my aunt...it has been in my family at least thirty years. When my garden grows more cucumbers than I need, I make this recipe to share with friends.

3 to 4 cucumbers, peeled and sliced
3/4 c. mayonnaise-style salad dressing

1/2 c. sugar
1/4 c. white vinegar
salt and pepper to taste
Optional: 1 onion, thinly sliced

Place cucumbers in a serving bowl. Mix together remaining ingredients except onion and pour over cucumbers. Mix well. Fold in onion, if desired. Cover and refrigerate several hours before serving. Makes 6 to 8 servings.

German Cucumber Salad

Edie DeSpain
Logan, UT

My mother & father grew a large garden each year with lots of cucumbers, tomatoes, parsley, onions and fresh dill. I cherish Mother's old recipe which incorporates all of these vegetables.

1 cucumber, thinly sliced
1 onion, thinly sliced
1 tomato, thinly sliced
2 T. fresh parsley, minced
1/2 c. sour cream
3 T. fresh dill, minced

2 T. cider vinegar
2 T. milk
1/2 t. mustard
1/4 t. salt
pepper to taste

In a large serving bowl, combine cucumber, onion, tomato and parsley. Combine remaining ingredients; pour over cucumber mixture and stir well. Cover and chill at least one hour. Serves 4 to 6.

German-Style Spinach

Arden Regnier
East Moriches, NY

My grandmother said this recipe came from her mother, who received it from her own mother and brought it from Germany in 1863. It's the only way my daughters would eat spinach, and now they carry on this delicious tradition in their own homes.

2 slices bacon
2 T. all-purpose flour
2 27-oz. cans spinach, drained

garlic powder to taste
1 egg, hard-boiled, peeled and diced

In a skillet over medium heat, cook bacon until crisp. Remove bacon to a paper towel, reserving 2 tablespoons drippings in skillet. Add flour; cook and stir until flour starts to turn dark golden. Press out as much liquid from spinach as possible; add spinach and garlic powder to skillet. Heat through, stirring often, until thickened. Garnish with crumbled bacon and diced egg; serve as is or toss to mix. Makes 6 to 8 servings.

A vintage-style salad that's ready to serve in seconds! Top crisp wedges of iceberg lettuce with Thousand Island salad dressing, diced tomato and bacon crumbles. Yum!

Minted Zucchini Ribbons

Carrie O'Shea
Marina Del Rey, CA

My five-year-old daughter and I love making this delicious recipe together. She enjoys making the zucchini ribbons and helping me pick mint from our backyard herb garden.

1 lb. zucchini, trimmed
1 T. olive oil
2 cloves garlic, crushed

1/2 t. salt
2 T. fresh mint, chopped

With a vegetable peeler, peel long thin ribbons from each zucchini and set aside. In a skillet, heat oil over medium heat; add garlic and cook until golden. Discard garlic, reserving oil in skillet. Increase heat to medium-high; add zucchini and salt. Cook and stir just until zucchini wilts, about 2 minutes. Stir in mint before serving. Serves 4.

To show a child what once delighted you,
to find the child's delight added to your own,
this is happiness.

-J.B. Priestley

Cracker-Stuffed Squash

Denise Jones
Fountain, FL

My mother always made this yummy side dish and I loved it...it's the
only way I would eat squash as a youngster. Now that I'm older and
wiser, I'll eat delicious squash almost any way it's cooked...but Mother's
way is still a favorite!

5 yellow squash, trimmed
1 T. butter
2 eggs, beaten
2 c. saltine cracker crumbs

garlic powder, salt and pepper
   to taste
2 T. water
Optional: 1/2 c. onion, chopped

Place whole squash in a large saucepan with just enough water to
cover. Bring to a boil over medium-high heat. Reduce heat and
simmer 7 minutes, until tender. Drain and cool. Melt butter in a skillet
over medium heat. Cut squash in half lengthwise and scoop out
insides into skillet. Add remaining ingredients; cook and stir until
golden. Stuff squash halves with cracker mixture; arrange in a lightly
greased 3-quart casserole dish. Pour water into the bottom of the dish.
Bake, uncovered, at 325 degrees for 25 to 30 minutes, until golden.
Makes 10 servings.

Use seed packet clippings to embellish a small notebook...oh-so
handy for making shopping lists or keeping schedules.

Crispy French Fried Parsnips

Bev Fisher
Mesa, AZ

My mom knew how important it was to get us to eat veggies and looked for new ways to serve them. We found we liked this way!

2 lbs. parsnips, peeled and cut
   into strips
3 T. olive oil

1/2 t. sea salt or garlic salt
chili powder to taste

Toss parsnip strips in oil. Place on ungreased baking sheets and sprinkle with seasonings. Bake at 350 degrees for 30 minutes, turning halfway through, until tender. Makes 6 to 8 servings.

Seasoned Sweet Potato Fries

Cynthia Schwenk
East Greenville, PA

A healthier version of French fries that my family loves...the sweet potatoes are yummy! For extra crispness, broil before serving.

1/4 c. olive oil
1 t. Italian seasoning

3 sweet potatoes, cut into strips

Coat a 15"x10" jelly-roll pan with oil and seasoning. Add sweet potatoes and toss well. Bake at 375 degrees for 45 minutes to one hour, turning occasionally, until tender. Makes 4 to 6 servings.

Post a notepad on the fridge to make a note whenever a pantry staple is used up...you'll never run out of that one item you need.

Fried Dill Pickle Coins

Maria Hostettler
Fredonia, PA

*We tried these crunchy pickles at a restaurant and later
found the recipe. They're a family favorite!*

2 c. all-purpose flour
1/2 t. salt
1/4 t. pepper
2 eggs, beaten

1 c. milk
3 c. dill pickles, thinly sliced
oil for deep frying
Garnish: ranch salad dressing

In a bowl, combine flour, salt and pepper. In a separate bowl, whisk
eggs and milk together. Blot pickles well with paper towels. Coat
pickles with flour mixture, then with egg mixture. In a large deep
fryer, heat oil to 375 degrees. Add pickles, about 10 at a time, and
cook for 3 minutes, or until golden, turning once. Drain on paper
towels. Serve warm with ranch dressing. Serves 6.

Fried Green Tomatoes

Cathy Callen
Lawton, OK

*My mom grew up poor in Oklahoma during the Depression, so nothing
was wasted. When the weather turned cool, the last tomatoes were
gathered from the garden and fried or made into chow-chow relish. For
the crispest texture, make sure the tomatoes are still firm...if they've
begun to ripen, they won't fry well.*

1/2 c. cornmeal
1/2 c. all-purpose flour
1 t. salt
pepper to taste

4 to 6 green tomatoes, sliced
1/4-inch thick
1/2 c. canola oil

Mix cornmeal, flour, salt and pepper together in a shallow bowl.
Dredge tomatoes in mixture. Heat oil in a large skillet over medium
heat. Add tomatoes to skillet and cook until golden, turning once,
3 to 5 minutes on each side. Drain on paper towels. Serves about 6.

Wanda & Vickie's Baked Beans
Wanda Sidebottom
Lake Ozark, MO

*When I was in trade school, one of the students brought in this recipe
to share with everyone. My late daughter, Vickie, and I used to
serve this recipe at all kinds of parties.*

1 lb. brown & serve pork
    sausage links, cut into
    bite-size pieces
1 green pepper, chopped
1 onion, chopped
2 28-oz. cans pork & beans

1 c. catsup
1/4 c. brown sugar, packed
2 T. Worcestershire sauce
1 T. smoke-flavored cooking
    sauce
1/2 to 1 t. hot pepper sauce

In a skillet over medium-high heat, brown sausage links. Drain; add
green pepper and onion. Reduce heat to low; cook until onion is
translucent, about 2 minutes. Transfer to a 13"x9" baking pan sprayed
lightly with non-stick vegetable spray. Add remaining ingredients
and mix well; cover with aluminum foil. Bake at 375 degrees for
45 minutes to one hour. Serves 6 to 8.

Just for fun, hang a collection of old-fashioned straw garden hats
on wooden pegs by the kitchen door...maybe even
one that belonged to Mom or Grandma!

Sides & *Salads*

6-Bean Casserole

Angie Hamey
Somerville, OH

This is my go-to dish for potluck dinners and socials. It's a variation on plain ol' baked beans which everyone likes. This is even good as a main, served over a bed of rice.

2 16-oz. cans pork & beans
16-oz. can pinto beans
16-oz. can lima beans
16-oz. can butter beans
16-oz. can black beans or
　　black-eyed peas
4 onions, sliced and separated
　　into rings

1/2 c. vinegar
1 c. brown sugar, packed
1 t. garlic, minced
1/2 t. chili powder or 1 jalapeño
　　pepper, chopped

Pour pork & beans and pinto beans, including liquid, into a greased 13"x9" baking pan. Drain remaining beans in a colander; add to baking pan. Top with onion rings and set aside. In a small saucepan, mix together remaining ingredients. Bring to a boil over medium-high heat. Reduce heat to low; simmer for 20 minutes. Pour vinegar mixture over all. Cover and bake at 350 degrees for about 90 minutes. Serves 10 to 12.

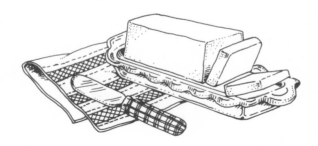

Make herbed butter in a jiffy...scrumptious on warm bread or melting into mashed potatoes. Unwrap a stick of butter and cut it in half lengthwise. Roll each half in finely chopped fresh parsley, rosemary, chives and thyme, then slice and serve.

BLT Salad with Basil Dressing

Nancy Willis
Farmington Hills, MI

My daughter and I like to go to our local farmers' market each Saturday morning. Together we buy fresh, ripe tomatoes, lettuce and basil for this salad, then go home and make it...enjoy!

1 lb. romaine lettuce, torn
1 pt. cherry tomatoes, quartered
1/2 lb. bacon, crisply cooked
   and crumbled, 2 T. drippings
   reserved

1/2 c. mayonnaise
2 T. red wine vinegar
1/4 c. fresh basil, chopped

In a large salad bowl, combine lettuce, tomatoes and crumbled bacon; set aside. In a small bowl, whisk together reserved drippings, mayonnaise, vinegar and basil. Drizzle dressing over salad and toss well. Top with Homemade Croutons and serve immediately. Makes 4 servings.

Homemade Croutons:

4 slices French bread, cubed
1 t. salt

1 t. pepper
1 T. olive oil

In a skillet over medium heat, toss bread cubes with salt and pepper. Drizzle with oil; toss and cook until golden.

Toss some candied pecans or walnuts over a salad for a special touch...terrific for nibbling too! Whisk one egg white with one teaspoon cold water and toss a pound of nuts in this mixture. Mix one cup sugar, one teaspoon cinnamon and 1/2 teaspoon salt; coat the nuts well. Spread nuts on a greased baking sheet. Bake at 225 degrees for one hour, stirring once or twice. Store in an airtight container.

Chopped Tomato Salad

Laurel Liebrecht
Yakima, WA

One evening while I was making dinner, my youngest son asked if he could add Kalamata olives to our usual salad, and it grew from there! The dressing is delicious on lots of other salads too.

4 tomatoes, chopped
1 red onion, thinly sliced
1 English cucumber, sliced and
    chopped

1/2 c. Kalamata olives, pitted
    and halved
1/3 c. fresh basil, shredded
Garnish: crumbled feta cheese

In a large salad bowl, combine all ingredients except feta cheese. Drizzle with Vinaigrette Dressing; toss to coat. Cover and refrigerate at least one hour, tossing once, until flavors are well blended. At serving time, sprinkle with cheese. Serves 4 to 6.

Vinaigrette Dressing:

5 T. red wine vinegar
4 t. olive oil
2 t. Dijon mustard

1/2 t. salt
1/2 t. pepper

Whisk together ingredients in a small bowl.

For an easy beginning to a savory meal, set out a piping-hot loaf of Italian bread and a little dish of olive oil sprinkled with Italian seasoning for dipping.

Sweet Creamed Tomatoes

Lena Smith
Pickerington, OH

When my daughter was born, my mother and my aunt came to stay for a week. They promised to cook whatever foods I wanted to eat. I hadn't eaten creamed tomatoes since I left home, so that's what I asked for. It was a perfect choice...so comforting!

1 loaf sourdough bread, sliced
    1-inch thick
3 T. olive oil
salt to taste

2 28-oz. cans stewed tomatoes
1/2 c. butter
1 c. milk
1/4 c. sugar

Lay bread slices on a baking sheet; brush with oil and sprinkle with salt. Broil for 2 to 3 minutes, until golden. Cool slightly. In a saucepan over medium-high heat, mix undrained tomatoes, butter, milk and sugar. Bring to a boil. Boil for one to 2 minutes, stirring frequently; remove from heat. To serve, place one to 2 slices of bread onto each dinner plate and ladle tomato mixture over top. Serve immediately. Makes 6 to 8 servings.

Green Beans & Tomatoes

Beth Garrison
Greenwood, IN

A friend of mine brought over this dish after the birth of our daughter, Kristen. I loved it so much I asked her for the recipe. It's become a favorite at family gatherings.

2 14-oz. cans green beans
14-oz. can diced or stewed
    tomatoes
1 onion, diced
1 green pepper, diced

2 T. Worcestershire sauce
1 T. brown sugar, packed
6 slices bacon, crisply cooked
    and crumbled

In a saucepan over medium heat, combine undrained beans and tomatoes with remaining ingredients except bacon. Stir and simmer until heated through. Add bacon just before serving. Makes 6 to 8 servings.

Marinated Brussels Sprouts

Penny Sherman
Cumming, GA

Every Saturday morning during the fall, my mother, daughters
and I visit the local farmers' market. We can't resist making these
when fresh Brussels sprouts are in season...yum!

1 lb. Brussels sprouts, trimmed
1/2 c. oil
1/4 c. vinegar

1/2 t. garlic powder
1/2 t. mustard
1/2 t. pepper

In a saucepan over medium-high heat, place Brussels sprouts with just enough water to cover. Boil for about 7 minutes, until just barely tender; drain. In a separate bowl, whisk together remaining ingredients. Pour over cooked sprouts while still warm; toss gently to coat. Cover and refrigerate 4 hours before serving. Makes 4 to 6 servings.

Let the kids help with meals...a sure way to get them interested in healthy choices! Younger children can fold napkins or tear lettuce for salad...older kids can measure, chop, stir and take part in meal planning and shopping. They may surprise you!

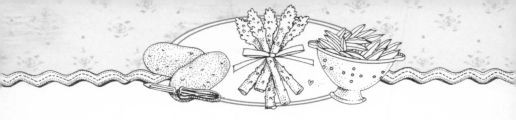

Roasted Asparagus

Sherry Carrier
Kenduskeag, ME

This is an easy, handed-down family favorite. It's super-simple and delicious! Try it with other veggies too.

1 lb. asparagus, trimmed	1/2 t. salt
1-1/2 T. olive oil	

Arrange asparagus in an aluminum foil-lined 13"x9" baking pan. Drizzle with oil; sprinkle with salt. Toss to coat asparagus evenly. Bake, uncovered, at 425 degrees for 10 to 15 minutes. Serves 4.

Cheesy Asparagus

Suzanne Stroud
Duncan, OK

One of the first recipes I got from my mother-in-law...it's the one & only way I'll eat asparagus!

15-oz. can asparagus spears, drained and juice reserved	12-oz. pkg. pasteurized process cheese spread, diced

Arrange asparagus in a lightly greased one-quart casserole dish; set aside. In a small saucepan, warm reserved juice and cheese over low heat, stirring often. Be careful not to burn. Once cheese is melted, pour over asparagus and bake, uncovered, at 350 degrees for 20 to 25 minutes, until bubbly and lightly golden. Serves 4.

Yummy Plum Dumplings

Andrea Ford
Montfort, WI

*A delicious and unusual side dish for roast pork...the recipe makes its
own sauce! My mom used to make this all the time, and now I do too.
The amount of water sounds like a lot, but it is correct.*

4 c. plums, pitted and halved
4 c. all-purpose flour
1 T. baking powder
1 t. salt

2 c. milk
3 to 4 c. water
1/2 c. butter, diced
2 c. sugar

Arrange plum halves in the bottom of a lightly greased 13"x9" baking
pan; set aside. In a bowl, combine flour, baking powder, salt and milk;
stir until dough forms. Pat dough evenly over plums. Pour enough
water down the side of dough to just reach the top of dough. Dot with
butter; sprinkle with sugar. Bake, uncovered, at 350 degrees for
1-1/2 hours. Serve warm. Makes 8 to 10 servings.

Need to clean baked-on food from a casserole dish? Place a dryer
sheet in the dish and fill with warm water. Let the dish stand
overnight, then sponge clean. You'll find the fabric softener
will really soften the baked-on food.

Simple Cottage Cheese Salad

Janet Coleman
Verona, OH

Everyone at our family reunions loves this salad of my mom's...even those who think they don't like cottage cheese!

16-oz. container cream-style
   cottage cheese
1/4 c. mayonnaise-style salad
   dressing

2 T. sugar
1 c. carrots, peeled and grated
1/2 c. green onions, chopped

In a salad bowl, stir together all ingredients. Serve immediately or cover and chill until serving time. Makes 6 to 8 servings.

A relish tray of crunchy bite-size vegetables like baby carrots, cherry tomatoes, broccoli flowerets and celery stalks is always welcome. Whip up a creamy dip for veggies by combining one cup cottage cheese, 1/4 cup plain yogurt, one tablespoon minced onion, one teaspoon dried parsley and 1/4 teaspoon dill weed. Blend until smooth and chill to allow flavor to develop.

Sweet Ambrosia

Sammie Warwick
Gulf Shores, AL

My mother-in-law shared this recipe for this old favorite with me. My husband enjoys it so much, I have to set aside a bowl just for him to enjoy later! It is a fast, easy dish that everyone likes.

16-oz. container low-fat frozen whipped topping, thawed
15-oz. can pineapple tidbits, drained
15-oz. can fruit cocktail, drained
10-oz. jar maraschino cherries, drained

8-oz. can mandarin oranges, drained
2 c. chopped walnuts
10-1/2 oz. pkg. mini marshmallows
1 c. sweetened flaked coconut

Spoon whipped topping into a large serving bowl. Add remaining ingredients and mix well. Cover and refrigerate at least one hour before serving. Makes 10 to 15 servings.

Carrying a salad to a picnic or potluck? Mix it up in a plastic zipping bag instead of a bowl, seal and set it right in the cooler. No worries about spills or leaks!

Honeyed Mango Salad

Phyl Broich Wessling
Garner, IA

We love this simple fruit-filled salad...it's yummy, quick & easy.

2 mangoes, pitted and sliced
2 oranges, segmented
1 banana, sliced
juice of 1 lime
2 T. honey

1/4 c. oil
1/8 t. salt
Garnish: 6 lettuce leaves,
    6 maraschino cherries

Combine fruit and lemon juice in a large bowl; toss to coat. Cover and chill until serving time. Blend lime juice and honey in a small bowl; stir in oil and salt. Drizzle honey mixture over fruit mixture; stir gently. To serve, place lettuce leaves in individual salad bowls; fill with fruit mixture. Top with cherries and any fruit juice remaining in bowl. Serves 6.

The bright colors of fresh fruit really shine in an antique cut-glass bowl. When washing cut glass, add a little white vinegar to the rinse water...the glass will sparkle!

Main Dishes

Mom's Slumgully

Denise Preston
Reading, OH

Mom used to make this one-pot wonder with its
funny name...we all loved it!

16-oz. pkg. shell macaroni,
   uncooked
2 lbs. ground beef
1 onion, chopped

4 stalks celery, chopped
2 10-oz. cans diced tomatoes
   with green chiles
salt and pepper to taste

Cook macaroni as package directs; drain and set aside. Meanwhile, in a large skillet over medium heat, brown beef, onion and celery. Drain; add salt and pepper to taste. Stir in tomatoes with juice and simmer for several minutes. Add cooked macaroni; reduce heat to low. Simmer for 10 to 15 minutes, stirring occasionally, until heated through. Serves 6 to 8.

Toss cooked pasta with a little olive oil, then set aside and keep warm. When it's time to add the pasta to a favorite recipe, you'll find the oil has kept the pasta from sticking together.

Cheesy Pizza Fondue

Tara Reiter-Marolf
Granger, IA

My mom would make this recipe for very special occasions when we had guests over to visit...a taste takes me right back to my childhood! My sister and I got to help out by toasting the muffins.

1/2 lb. ground beef
1 onion, chopped
2 8-oz. cans pizza sauce
1 T. cornstarch
1-1/2 t. dried oregano
1/4 t. garlic powder

1-1/4 c. shredded Cheddar
 cheese
1 c. shredded mozzarella cheese
6 English muffins, toasted
 and cubed

In a skillet over medium heat, brown beef with onion; drain. Stir in pizza sauce, cornstarch and seasonings. Add cheeses 1/3 at a time, stirring until melted. Pour mixture into a fondue pot to keep warm. Serve with toasted English muffin cubes for dipping. Serves 6.

When chopping onions or celery, it only takes a moment to chop a little extra. Tuck them away in the freezer for a quick start to dinner another day.

Alabama Chicken Casserole

Betty Lou Wright
Hendersonville, TN

Every time I make this casserole, I think of my precious mother-in-law, Virginia, who introduced me to it. If I had a nickel for every time it has graced our table or has been carried to a potluck, I'd be a wealthy woman! Now I use reduced-fat mayo and soup and omit the egg yolks for a heart-healthier dish...it's still scrumptious!

2 to 3 c. cooked chicken, chopped
4 eggs, hard-boiled, peeled and chopped
2 c. cooked rice
1-1/2 c. celery, chopped
1 onion, chopped

2 10-3/4 oz. cans cream of mushroom soup
1 c. mayonnaise
2 T. lemon juice
3-oz. pkg. slivered almonds
5-oz. can chow mein noodles

Mix all ingredients except noodles in a large bowl. Transfer to a greased 13"x9" baking pan. Cover and refrigerate overnight. Uncover and bake at 350 degrees for one hour, or until hot and bubbly. Top with noodles; return to oven for 5 minutes. Makes 10 to 12 servings.

Mom's best recipes usually make lots of servings, perfect for sharing. Invite a neighbor or a co-worker that you'd like to get to know better...encourage your kids to invite a friend. You're sure to have a great time together!

Mom's Cola Chicken

Carla Slajchert
Minot AFB, ND

Growing up, we knew Mom would be making this delicious, tender chicken when we saw her get out the electric skillet. She likes simple recipes with just a few ingredients...they always manage to taste like so much more!

1-1/2 lbs. boneless, skinless chicken breasts	salt and pepper to taste
Optional: 1 to 2 T. oil	20-oz. bottle cola, divided
	1 to 2 c. catsup, divided

Arrange chicken in an ungreased, non-stick electric skillet or a skillet on the stovetop, using oil if skillet isn't non-stick. Sprinkle chicken with salt and pepper. Pour enough cola over chicken to cover it; pour one cup catsup over chicken, adding a little at a time until mixture thickens a little. Cover and cook over medium heat for about 45 minutes, adding remaining cola and catsup a little at a time, every 10 to 15 minutes. Cook an additional 45 minutes, until chicken juices run clear. Serves 4.

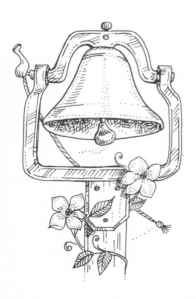

Start a new family tradition...call everyone in to dinner by ringing a dinner bell! You can even let the kids take turns on different nights.

Linguine in Clam Sauce

Cora Wilfinger
Manitowoc, WI

This recipe has been in my family for nearly twenty-five years and my kids still ask for it all the time...it's that good! You may even want to double it, to make plenty for second helpings.

10-oz. pkg. linguine pasta, uncooked
1/4 c. olive oil
3 cloves garlic, minced
1/4 c. water
2 T. butter, sliced
1/2 t. fresh parsley, chopped
1/4 t. dried oregano
1/2 t. salt
1/4 t. pepper
6-1/2 oz. can chopped clams

Cook pasta as package directs; drain and set aside. Meanwhile, combine oil and garlic in a skillet over medium heat; stir until lightly golden. Carefully add water; stir in butter and seasonings. Stir until butter melts; slowly add undrained clams. Simmer for a few minutes, until heated through. Serve over cooked pasta. Serves 4 to 5.

Lemon Herb & Garlic Shrimp

Cherylann Smith
Efland, NC

This shrimp dish is often requested by my children....and when Daddy isn't looking, they sneak shrimp off his plate!

2 cloves garlic, pressed
2 T. olive oil
6 T. butter, sliced
1 lb. frozen cooked shrimp
1.8-oz. pkg. lemon herb soup mix
1 c. warm water

In a skillet over medium heat, sauté garlic in olive oil and butter for 2 minutes. Add shrimp and simmer until shrimp thaws, stirring often. Dissolve soup mix in water; pour over shrimp mixture. Reduce heat; simmer until heated through, about 20 minutes. Makes 4 to 6 servings.

Evelyn's Crab-Stuffed Potatoes

Diane Brulc
Brookfield, WI

*Mom always cooked the most delicious food. She would make
these potatoes for us as a special treat.*

4 baking potatoes
1/2 c. butter, sliced and softened
1/4 c. light cream
salt to taste
1/8 t. pepper

4 t. onion, grated
1 c. shredded sharp Cheddar
  cheese
6-1/2 oz. can crabmeat, drained
1/2 t. paprika

Place potatoes on an ungreased baking sheet. Bake at 325 degrees
for about 50 minutes, until partially tender. Remove from oven;
pierce potatoes with a fork and return to oven. Bake an additional
50 minutes, until tender. Cut baked potatoes in half lengthwise. Scoop
out potato pulp into a large bowl; return potato skins to baking sheet
and set aside. Add butter, cream, salt, pepper, onion and cheese to
potato pulp; whip until mixed. Fold in crabmeat with a fork. Spoon
mixture into potato skins; sprinkle with paprika. Bake, uncovered, at
450 degrees for 15 minutes, until heated through. Serves 4.

For the fluffiest baked potatoes, use a fork to pierce them twice at
the center, forming an X. Gently press the potatoes at both ends
and they will pop open. Mmm...pass the butter, please!

Cowboy Macaroni & Cheese

Linda McWilliams
Fillmore, NY

*Ahhh, comfort food. When my children were little they were picky
eaters. I found they would try new recipes if I gave them
special names. This name did the trick...they ate it up!*

3 c. elbow macaroni, uncooked
10-3/4 oz. can cream of
 mushroom soup
1/2 c. milk
1/2 t. dry mustard

pepper to taste
3 c. shredded Cheddar cheese,
 divided
Optional: 4 hot dogs, diced
2 c. French fried onions, divided

Cook macaroni according to package directions; drain and set aside.
Blend soup, milk, mustard and pepper; stir in cooked macaroni, hot
dogs if using and 2 cups cheese. Sprinkle with half the onions and
mix well. Transfer to a 13"x9" baking pan sprayed with non-stick
vegetable spray. Cover; bake at 400 degrees for 30 minutes. Remove
from oven; top with remaining cheese and onions. Serves 6 to 8.

Famous White Mac & Cheese

Shannon James
Georgetown, KY

*When my four kids come running in from playing and see that my
mac & cheese is in the oven, it puts a smile on everyone's face.*

16-oz. pkg. elbow macaroni,
 uncooked
2 T. butter
2 T. all-purpose flour
3 c. milk

1 lb. Monterey Jack cheese,
 cubed
1/2 lb. Pepper Jack cheese,
 cubed

Cook macaroni as package directs; drain and set aside. Meanwhile,
melt butter in a saucepan over medium heat. Stir in flour until
combined; add milk and stir until mixture boils. Remove from heat.
Add cheese and stir until melted. Combine hot mixture with cooked
macaroni; place in an ungreased 13"x9" baking pan. Bake, uncovered,
at 350 degrees for 30 minutes. Makes 8 servings.

Saucy Beef & Macaroni

Cathy McNabb
Moore, OK

This casserole is one that my mom made often. It's quick and uses common pantry ingredients. This is my interpretation of her family favorite...it even tastes great reheated!

2 c. elbow macaroni, uncooked
1 lb. ground beef
1/2 c. onion, chopped
1/4 c. celery, chopped
1/4 c. green pepper, chopped

1 T. garlic, minced
28-oz. can stewed tomatoes
15-oz. can tomato sauce
6-oz. can tomato paste
salt and pepper to taste

Cook macaroni according to package directions; drain and set aside. In a skillet over medium heat, brown beef, onion, celery, green pepper and garlic; drain. Add remaining ingredients to skillet; simmer for 10 minutes. Combine beef mixture with cooked macaroni and spoon into a lightly greased 2-quart casserole dish. Bake, uncovered, at 350 degrees for 35 to 40 minutes, until hot and bubbly. Makes 6 to 8 servings.

Use Mom's vintage casserole dishes from the 1960s to serve up casseroles with sweet memories. If you don't have any of her dishes, keep an eye open at tag sales and thrift stores...you may find the very same style she used!

Blue-Ribbon Corn Dog Bake

Tiffani Schulte
Wyandotte, MI

My kids love, love, love corn dogs, but I never have the time to make the real deal. One day I decided to give an old favorite, my mom's cornbread recipe, a new twist by adding hot dogs. The result was a hit at our house! This casserole is oh-so easy and it really does taste like a county fair corn dog.

1/3 c. sugar
1 egg, beaten
1 c. all-purpose flour
3/4 T. baking powder
1/2 t. salt

1/2 c. yellow cornmeal
1/2 T. butter, melted
3/4 c. milk
16-oz. pkg. hot dogs, sliced into
    bite-size pieces

In a small bowl, mix together sugar and egg. In a separate bowl, mix together flour, baking powder and salt. Add flour mixture to sugar mixture. Add cornmeal, butter and milk, stirring just to combine. Stir in hot dogs. Pour into a well-greased 8"x8" baking pan. Bake, uncovered, at 375 degrees for about 15 minutes, or until a toothpick inserted near the center comes out clean. Serves 6.

Small-town county fairs, food festivals, swap meets...the list
goes on and on, so grab a friend (or two!) and go for
good old-fashioned fun!

Hot Dog Burreenies

Martha Stephens
Sibley, LA

When I was going to night school, my husband was in charge of making supper for our daughters. They're very fond of hot dogs, so he came up with this creation for them...they like it too!

5 hot dogs, cooked and sliced
   into bite-size pieces
8 to 10 8-inch flour tortillas,
   warmed

2 to 3 c. shredded Cheddar
   cheese, divided
1/4 c. grated Parmesan cheese

Arrange 1/2 sliced hot dog in the center of each tortilla; sprinkle 1/3 cup Cheddar cheese evenly over hot dog. Roll up tortillas and place seam-side down in a greased 13"x9" baking pan. Lightly sprinkle tops with Parmesan cheese and remaining Cheddar cheese. Bake, uncovered, at 300 degrees for about 10 minutes, or until cheese is melted. Makes about 6 servings.

Make a game of table talk! Write fun questions on file cards...what kind of animal would you like to be? What's your favorite storybook? What's your favorite time of year? and so on. Pull a different card each night to talk about.

Anita's Onion Steaks

Anita Mullins
Eldridge, MO

A simply delicious way to fix budget-friendly cube steaks!
Serve them with mashed potatoes, cooked egg noodles or rice,
with the gravy from the skillet ladled over all.

15-oz. can beef broth
Optional: 1/2 c. red wine
1.35-oz. pkg. onion soup mix
1 onion, thinly sliced

4 beef cube steaks
pepper to taste
10-3/4 oz. can cream of onion
   soup

In a skillet over medium heat, combine broth, wine if desired and soup mix; mix well. Add onion and steaks; sprinkle with pepper to taste. Reduce heat to low; cover and simmer for 30 minutes. Turn steaks over; cover and simmer for an additional 30 minutes. Remove steaks to a plate; stir soup into mixture in skillet. Return steaks to skillet, being sure to coat each steak with gravy. Cover and simmer over low heat for 15 minutes longer. Serves 4.

Whip up some whimsical magnets for the fridge. Buy self-adhesive magnetic sheets at a photo shop, peel off the backs and stick on photos of your children, friends and pets. The figures in the photos can even be cut out for clever shaped photo magnets.

Steak San Marco

Darlene Nolen
Whittier, NC

I found this recipe in our local newspaper over twenty years ago.
It has become a favorite of our family, especially my youngest
son, Rick. Substitute beef skirt steak, if you like.

1 lb. beef round steak, sliced
   into thin strips
1 T. oil
1.35-oz. pkg. onion soup mix

28-oz. can diced tomatoes
3 T. cider vinegar
cooked rice

In a skillet over medium heat, brown beef in oil; drain. Add soup mix
to beef; mix well. Stir in tomatoes with juice and vinegar. Bring to a
low boil and stir until mixed. Reduce heat; cover and simmer for one
hour or until beef is tender, stirring occasionally. Serve over cooked
rice. Serves 4 to 6.

Scenic vintage souvenir plates are fun to find at flea markets.
They're sure-fire conversation starters at the dinner table too! Look
for ones from your home state or from favorite vacation spots.

Daddy's Shepherd's Pie

Sheila Wakeman
Winnsboro, TX

*My dad grew up eating this dish. I can remember going to Dad's house
on the weekends (he was a single dad) and we would make this
together. Now my daughter and I make it together too.*

1 lb. ground beef
10-3/4 oz. can cream of
   mushroom soup
2/3 c. water
7.2-oz. pkg. homestyle creamy
   butter-flavored instant
   mashed potato flakes

2 c. corn
8-oz. pkg. shredded Cheddar
   cheese

Brown beef in a skillet over medium heat; drain. Stir in soup and
water; simmer until heated through. Meanwhile, prepare potato flakes
as package directs; set aside. Place beef mixture in a 13"x9" baking
pan sprayed with non-stick vegetable spray. Top with corn; spread
potatoes evenly across top. Sprinkle with cheese. Bake, uncovered,
at 425 degrees for about 10 minutes, until hot and cheese is melted.
Makes 6 to 8 servings.

Mashed Potato Pie

Laurie Kunigel
Schenectady, NY

*A one-dish meal that my mom used to make...it always tasted so good
after I'd been playing outside in the snow all day!*

1 lb. ground beef, browned
   and drained
10-3/4 oz. can tomato soup

14-1/2 oz. can French-style
   green beans, drained
2 to 3 c. mashed potatoes

Combine beef, soup and beans in an ungreased 2-quart casserole dish.
Spread potatoes over top. Bake, uncovered, at 350 degrees for 20 to
30 minutes, until potatoes are lightly golden. Serves 6.

Mom's Secret Stew

Denise Ross
Jefferson, MA

My husband and son really enjoy this slow-cooker stew. My son even asked for the recipe now that he's on his own. He said it came out real good when he made it...of course, he prefers it spicier!

1 lb. stew beef, cubed	2 to 3 T. all-purpose flour
2 to 3 T. olive oil	2 potatoes, chopped
1 c. beef broth	1 turnip, peeled and chopped
2 T. Worcestershire sauce	1 onion, chopped
1/4 c. molasses	2 carrots, peeled and sliced
1/4 c. catsup	1/2 red-hot chile pepper,
1 t. dried marjoram	chopped
salt and pepper to taste	

In a skillet over medium heat, brown beef in oil. Remove beef to a slow cooker and set aside. Whisk broth into oil, scraping the bottom of the skillet to get all the brown bits at the bottom. Whisk in Worcestershire sauce, molasses, catsup and seasonings. Gradually whisk in small amounts of flour until thickened. Add vegetables to slow cooker and pour in broth mixture. Cover and cook on low setting for 8 hours, or on high setting for 6 hours. Serves 4.

On Saturday mornings, start a favorite dish in the slow cooker, then enjoy the day with your family. What a great way to take it easy!

Pasta Trapanese

Claudia Passaro
Chester, NJ

*We chose this delectable sauce for the pasta course at
our wedding dinner. It's a Sicilian recipe from my mom.*

12-oz. pkg. penne pasta,
   uncooked
1 onion, chopped
2 cloves garlic, crushed
1/4 c. olive oil
28-oz. can whole Italian plum
   tomatoes, crushed

5 to 6 T. fresh basil, chopped
salt and pepper to taste
1/4 c. slivered almonds, toasted
Optional: grated Parmesan
   cheese

Cook pasta as package directs; drain and set aside. Meanwhile, in a
skillet over medium heat, sauté onion and garlic in oil. Add tomatoes
with juice, basil, salt and pepper. Reduce heat and simmer, uncovered,
for 30 minutes. Stir in almonds. Serve over cooked pasta, topped with
Parmesan cheese, if desired. Serves 4.

Set a regular dinner theme for each night of the week...Italian Night,
Soup & Salad Night or Mexican Night, based on your family's
favorites. You'll be creating memories together...and meal
planning is a snap!

Kristin's Perfect Pizza

Kristin Stone
Davis, CA

My mom used to make this homemade pizza when I was a child and I adored it. Now that I'm an adult, I've perfected the no-cook sauce even more. You could also use the dough to make two smaller pizzas or even bread sticks...have fun with it!

3 c. bread flour
1 t. salt
1/2 t. sugar
1 c. warm water

1 T. oil
1 T. quick-rising yeast
Garnish: favorite pizza toppings

In a bowl, combine flour, salt and sugar. Heat water until very warm, about 110 to 115 degrees. Add water to bowl along with oil and yeast. Knead by hand for 3 minutes; form into a ball. Cover and let rise until double in size, about an hour. Punch down dough; let rest for 4 minutes. On a floured surface, roll out dough about 1/4-inch thick. Place on an ungreased 16" round pizza pan. Let rise an additional 10 to 15 minutes. Spread Pizza Sauce over dough; add desired toppings. Place in a cold oven; turn to 500 degrees. Bake for 17 to 20 minutes, until golden. Serves 6.

Pizza Sauce:

8-oz. can tomato sauce
6-oz. can tomato paste
1-1/4 t. dried oregano

1-1/4 t. dried basil
1-1/4 t. garlic powder
1 t. salt

Stir together ingredients in a medium bowl.

Mix up your own Italian seasoning to store in a big shaker jar...you probably already have the ingredients in your spice rack! A good basic blend is 2 tablespoons each of dried oregano, basil, thyme, marjoram and rosemary...add or subtract to suit your family's taste.

Peppered Pork Loin

Deanna Robinson
Robson, WV

This roast pork makes delicious sandwiches! Slice leftovers to desired thickness and fry in a skillet coated with non-stick vegetable spray.

1/2 t. pepper
1/2 t. garlic and pepper
   seasoning salt

1/2 t. Cajun seasoning
4 to 6-lb. boneless pork loin

Mix together seasonings and rub into pork loin. Wrap in 2 sheets of heavy-duty aluminum foil, sealing well. Place on a baking sheet. Bake at 350 degrees for 1-1/2 to 2 hours. Let stand 15 minutes before slicing. Makes 14 servings.

Country Pork Skillet

Lynda Robson
Boston, MA

This one-pot meal is on the table in less than 30 minutes. It's as good as it is easy...even my two picky boys will eat veggies this way!

4 boneless pork chops, diced
1 T. oil
12-oz. jar pork gravy

2 T. catsup
8 new redskin potatoes, diced
2 c. frozen mixed vegetables

In a skillet over medium heat, brown pork in oil; drain. Stir in gravy, catsup and potatoes; cover and simmer for 10 minutes. Stir in vegetables; cook an additional 10 to 15 minutes, until vegetables are tender. Serves 4.

Slice or dice uncooked meat in a jiffy...pop it in the freezer for 10 to 15 minutes first, until it's slightly frozen.

Main *Dishes*

Pork Chops Stroganoff Style

Andrea Ford
Montfort, WI

This was my mom's recipe...the flavor is unbelievably good!

4 pork chops, one-inch thick
2 T. oil
1 onion, sliced
16-oz. pkg. sliced mushrooms
1/4 c. water

2 t. mustard
1/2 t. salt
1/2 c. sour cream
Optional: cooked rice

In a skillet over medium-high heat, cook pork chops in oil until browned, about 2 minutes on each side. Remove to a plate. Add onion and mushrooms to drippings in skillet; cook until tender, stirring occasionally. Return pork chops to skillet. Add water, mustard and salt; heat to boiling. Reduce heat to low. Cover and simmer for one hour, or until chops are fork-tender. Remove chops to a warm platter. Stir sour cream into drippings in skillet until blended; heat through without boiling. To serve, spoon sauce over chops and cooked rice, if desired. Makes 4 servings.

The secret to tender steamed rice! Cook long-cooking rice according to package directions. When it's done, remove pan from heat, cover with a folded tea towel and put lid back on. Let stand for 5 to 10 minutes before serving. The towel will absorb any excess moisture.

Cordon Bleu Casserole

*Jackie Flood
Geneseo, NY*

I revised an old family recipe to create this one, and I wasn't sure my husband would like it. I needn't have worried! After serving this, I overheard him exclaiming to a neighbor about a terrific dinner we'd had recently...it was this recipe!

8-oz. pkg. penne pasta, uncooked
6-oz. pkg. spreadable creamy Swiss cheese wedges
1 c. fat-free half-and-half
1 t. butter-flavored granules
1 t. garlic salt
1/2 t. pepper
3/4 c. cooked chicken breast, diced
1/2 c. cooked ham, diced
Garnish: 1/4 c. shredded Swiss cheese, 1/8 c. seasoned dry bread crumbs

Cook pasta as package directs; drain and set aside. Meanwhile, in a large saucepan over medium-low heat, combine cheese wedges, half-and-half, butter-flavored granules, garlic salt and pepper. Cook, stirring often, until cheese is melted and smooth. Add chicken, ham and cooked pasta. Stir until well blended and heated through. Top with shredded cheese and bread crumbs at serving time. Serves 6.

Try using fat-free or reduced-fat dairy products like
sour cream, cream cheese and cheese in your favorite family
recipes. They're just as creamy and good but much better
for you than the full-fat versions.

Main *Dishes*

Easy Bowtie Lasagna

Sheila Murray
Tehachapi, CA

This casserole is delicious and it's so simple to put together.
Add a crisp green salad and garlic bread...dinner is ready!

16-oz. pkg. bowtie pasta,
   uncooked
1 lb. ground beef
1 onion, chopped
32-oz. jar spaghetti sauce

8-oz. container sour cream
1/4 c. grated Parmesan cheese
1 t. garlic powder
2 c. shredded mozzarella cheese

Cook pasta as package directs; drain and set aside. Meanwhile, in a
skillet over medium heat, brown beef and onion; drain. Add spaghetti
sauce to skillet and simmer for 5 minutes. Mix cooked pasta with sour
cream, Parmesan cheese and garlic powder. In a greased 13"x9" baking
pan, layer half of beef mixture and half of pasta mixture. Repeat
layers; top with mozzarella cheese. Bake, uncovered, at 350 degrees
for about 30 minutes, until heated through and cheese is melted.
Serves 6 to 8.

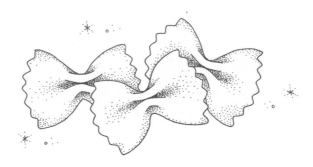

Children will love pasta dishes spooned into individual ramekins
or custard cups. Easy to serve and just their size!

Yummy Pork Ribs

Lee Beedle
Church View, VA

I enjoy trying new recipes and this is one I find myself recommending to everyone...it's delectable and oh-so-easy!

2 c. zesty Italian salad dressing
1/4 c. soy sauce
1 T. garlic, minced
1/2 t. pepper

3 to 4 lbs. bone-in country-style
   pork ribs or chops
2 T. olive oil
2 to 3 onions, sliced into rings

In a small bowl, stir together salad dressing, soy sauce, garlic and pepper; set aside. In a skillet over medium heat, brown ribs in oil on both sides; drain. Arrange onion rings in an ungreased 13"x9" baking pan. Top with ribs; drizzle dressing mixture over top. Cover tightly. Bake at 350 degrees for one hour, or until tender. Serves 6.

Oversized bandannas in a rainbow of colors make whimsical napkins...just right for messy-but-tasty foods like barbecued ribs, corn on the cob and wedges of juicy watermelon!

Melt-in-Your-Mouth Pork Chops

Renee Spec
Crescent, PA

An easy, economical slow-cooker meal that's very tasty.
My husband is happy to take any leftovers for his lunch.

4 pork loin chops
10-3/4 oz. can cream of celery
   soup
1-1/3 c. water

garlic salt and dried parsley
   to taste
cooked rice

Place pork chops in a slow cooker. Blend together soup, water and seasonings; spoon over pork chops. Cover and cook on low setting for 6 to 8 hours, or until pork is cooked through. Serve chops and gravy over cooked rice. Makes 4 servings.

A quick & easy side dish that's easy to toss together! Quarter new redskin potatoes and toss with a little olive oil, salt and pepper. Spread in a baking pan and bake at 400 degrees for 35 to 40 minutes, until crisp and golden.

Lemon-Teriyaki Glazed Chicken

Wendy Love
Hillsboro, OR

*My mother used to make this delicious dish for us kids when we were
growing up...I can still smell that wonderful aroma! I'll always cherish
how hard she worked to fill our lives with terrific memories.*

1/2 c. lemon juice
1/2 c. soy sauce
1/4 c. sugar
3 T. brown sugar, packed
2 T. water

4 cloves garlic, finely chopped
3/4 t. ground ginger
8 chicken thighs
Optional: steamed rice

In a large skillet, combine all ingredients except chicken and rice.
Cook over medium heat for 3 minutes; add chicken. Cover and simmer
over low heat for 30 minutes, or until tender, turning once. Serve with
steamed rice, if desired. Makes 4 servings.

Tangy BBQ Chicken

Jewel Sharpe
Raleigh, NC

*The barbecue sauce in this recipe is our family favorite...I could
almost drink it! The recipe makes about 1-1/2 cups sauce
that's tasty on chicken, beef and pork.*

1 c. brewed coffee
1 c. catsup
1/2 c. sugar
1/2 c. Worcestershire sauce

1/4 c. cider vinegar
1/8 t. pepper
8 chicken legs with thighs

In a saucepan, combine all ingredients except chicken. Bring to a boil
over medium heat; reduce heat to low. Simmer, uncovered, for 30 to
35 minutes until thickened, stirring occasionally. Grill chicken as
desired, brushing with sauce as it cooks. Makes 8 servings.

Main *Dishes*

Savory Hot Chicken & Rice

Jessica Branch
Colchester, IL

My mom used to make this hearty dish to send home with me when I was an intern...it fed my roommate and me all week. The water chestnuts and almonds add crunch and the pimentos add a dash of color. Thanks, Mom!

2 c. cooked chicken, diced
1-1/2 c. long-cooking rice, cooked
10-3/4 oz. can cream of chicken soup
1 c. mayonnaise
8-oz. can water chestnuts, drained and chopped
2-oz. jar diced pimentos, drained

1/2 c. slivered almonds
2 t. onion, finely chopped
2 t. lemon juice
1/2 t. salt
1/2 t. pepper
1 c. bread cubes
3 T. butter, melted
garlic salt to taste

In a large bowl, mix together all ingredients except bread, butter and garlic salt. Spread mixture in a greased 13"x9" baking pan. Toss bread with butter; spread on a baking sheet. Bake at 400 degrees for 15 to 20 minutes, stirring after 10 minutes, until golden. Add garlic salt to taste; sprinkle over chicken mixture. Bake, uncovered, at 350 degrees for 30 to 40 minutes, until hot and bubbly. Makes 6 to 8 servings.

When a recipe calls for cooked chicken, try poaching for juicy, tender chicken. Cover boneless, skinless chicken breasts with water in a saucepan. Bring to a boil, then turn down the heat, cover and simmer over low heat for 10 to 12 minutes. The chicken is done when it is no longer pink in the center.

Nana's Easy Pot Roast

Natalie Anstine
Canton, OH

This is my mother-in-law's slow-cooker roast. It's scrumptious...and I was shocked at how simple it is to make! Everyone in the family asks her to make this dish for their birthday meal. The soup and onion make a perfect gravy without having to add anything else!

2 to 3-lb. beef chuck roast
10-3/4 oz. can golden
    mushroom soup

1 sweet onion, thinly sliced

Place roast in a slow cooker. Pour soup over roast; top with onion slices. Cover and cook on low setting for 5 to 6 hours, until roast is tender. Serve with gravy from slow cooker. Makes 6 to 8 servings.

Everyone knows mashed potatoes are the perfect side dish for pot roast and gravy. Try a delicious secret the next time you fix the potatoes...substitute equal parts chicken broth and cream for the milk in any favorite recipe.

Slow-Cooker Rich Beef Stew

Jennifer Levy
Warners, NY

This recipe was given to me by my sister, Karen. We both make it often for family meals, and we're proud to serve it to company too! It's delicious...even our picky kids eat it and ask for seconds. Serve with crusty bread to enjoy all the scrumptious gravy.

2-1/2 lbs. stew beef, cubed
10-3/4 oz. can cream of
   mushroom soup
10-3/4 oz. can French onion
   soup

1 c. dry red wine or beef broth
4-oz. can sliced mushrooms,
   drained
cooked egg noodles

Combine all ingredients except noodles in a slow cooker. Stir to mix. Cover and cook on low setting for 8 to 10 hours. Serve over cooked egg noodles. Serves 6.

Inexpensive, less-tender cuts of beef like chuck roast and round steak become fork-tender and delicious after slow-cooking all day. Why not fix a double batch when they're on sale? You can shred leftovers for scrumptious, quick & easy tacos or burritos.

Sarah's Tuna Casserole Supreme

Tracey Regnold
Lewisville, TX

*This good old-fashioned dish started with my mother's recipe. My
daughter, Sarah, and I made it our own with a few tweaks. The
ingredients are usually in our pantry, so it's easy to make anytime.*

16-oz. pkg. wide egg noodles,
  uncooked
1 onion, chopped
1/2 c. celery, chopped
1 to 2 T. butter
2 6-oz. cans tuna, drained
10-3/4 oz. can cream of
  mushroom soup

10-3/4 oz. can golden
  mushroom soup
1/2 lb. pasteurized process
  cheese spread, cubed
15-1/4 oz. can peas, drained
1 c. shredded Cheddar cheese
1 c. potato chips, crushed
salt and pepper to taste

Cook noodles as package directs; drain and set aside. Meanwhile, in
a large skillet over medium heat, sauté onion and celery in butter
until translucent. Add cooked noodles to skillet; stir in tuna, soups
and cheese spread. Cook until blended and cheese is melted, one to
2 minutes. Stir in peas. Transfer to a lightly greased 13"x9" baking
pan; top with Cheddar cheese. Bake, uncovered, at 350 degrees for
20 to 25 minutes, until hot and bubbly. Top with crushed potato
chips. Return to oven and bake an additional 5 to 10 minutes, until
chips are golden. Makes 4 to 6 servings.

Fresh out of potato chips for this crunchy topping? Use herb-flavored
stuffing mix in their place and it'll be just as yummy!

Risotto Salmonato

Marsha Grove
Torrance, CA

I received this delicious recipe from a good Italian friend. When my daughter-in-law and I prepare this dish together, we put on the Italian music and cook away...we feel as if we're in Italy. A cooking tip...don't rinse the rice!

1/3 c. butter	1 to 2 c. fish broth or clam juice,
6 cloves garlic, minced	divided
16-oz. pkg. Arborio rice,	1 t. salt
uncooked	1/8 t. pepper
1-1/4 c. champagne, white wine	1 T. fresh parsley, chopped
or fish broth	1 c. whipping cream
3/4 lb. salmon fillet, chopped	

In a large saucepan over medium heat, melt butter. Add garlic and sauté slowly, until soft and golden. Add rice and stir well. Sauté for about 5 minutes. Add 1-1/4 cups champagne, wine or fish broth and salmon to skillet; bring to a boil. Reduce heat to low; cover and simmer. In a separate saucepan, heat fish broth or clam juice over low heat until warm. After mixture in skillet has simmered for 5 minutes, add 1/2 cup warmed broth or juice to skillet. Continue simmering, covered, about 20 to 25 minutes; add remaining broth every 5 minutes, 1/2 cup at a time, stirring after each addition. Add salt, pepper and parsley. Stir in cream; heat through for one to 2 minutes. Serves 6.

Large scallop shells make delightful serving containers for seafood dishes. Use shells you've found on a family vacation or check party supply stores for dinner-ready shells.

Meatless Nut Patties

Kara Azevedo
Fishers, IN

This recipe was shared with me by my mother-in-law...it took me ten years to figure out how she got these patties to turn out so yummy! Since she has passed on, I always make them for family gatherings. In my experience, an electric skillet works much better than a skillet on the stovetop.

6 slices bread, lightly toasted
4 to 5 T. olive oil, divided
2 eggs, beaten
1 t. poultry seasoning
1/2 c. onion, chopped
1 c. shredded Cheddar cheese
1/2 c. chopped walnuts or pecans
14-1/2 oz. can diced tomatoes, drained
14-1/2 oz. can diced tomatoes with chiles, drained

Tear bread into very small pieces and place in a large bowl. Add 3 tablespoons oil and remaining ingredients except tomatoes. Using your hands, mix until just combined; gently form into 8 patties. Patties will be slightly chunky. Heat an electric skillet to 375 degrees. As it begins to warm, add one to 2 tablespoons oil. Cook patties on one side for 3 to 4 minutes, until lightly golden; turn over and cook the other side. Spread tomatoes evenly over patties. Reduce heat to 210 to 215 degrees. Cover skillet and cook for 30 minutes. Remove lid; continue cooking for 15 minutes. Serve immediately. Serves 4.

Add some fresh broccoli or snow peas to a favorite pasta recipe...simply drop chopped veggies into the pasta pot about halfway through the cooking time. Pasta and veggies will be tender at about the same time.

Ricotta Gnocchi

Eleanor Dionne
Beverly, MA

This is my mother's recipe from more than forty years ago. She made all her pasta by hand. My children look forward to these each time I make it. Now my daughter has learned how to make these and my grandchildren can't wait to eat them. Very easy to do!

32-oz. container ricotta cheese
1 egg, beaten
1 t. salt

4 c. all-purpose flour, divided
Garnish: tomato sauce, grated
    Parmesan cheese

Combine ricotta, egg and salt in a large bowl; mix thoroughly with a large spoon. Gradually add flour, one cup at a time. When dough is no longer sticky, knead slightly on a lightly floured board. Break off chunks; roll into long ropes. Cut ropes into pieces the size of a cherry. Roll in a little flour with the back of a fork. Place on a clean tea towel to dry. To serve gnocchi, boil for 8 to 10 minutes in a large pot of salted water. Garnish with warmed tomato sauce and Parmesan cheese. Serves 6.

While dinner cooks, pop some Parmesan bread in the oven.
Blend 1/4 cup butter, 2 tablespoons grated Parmesan cheese,
2 teaspoons minced garlic and 1/4 teaspoon Italian seasoning.
Spread it over a halved loaf of French bread and broil until golden.

Sour Cream Chili Bake

Victoria Wright
Orland Park, IL

My mom shared this recipe with me when I was a teenager. I don't know if it was her own creation or not, but she made it her own! Whenever I make this dish I'm reminded of both my mom and of Arizona...I miss them both very much!

1 lb. ground turkey or beef
15-oz. can chili beans, drained
10-oz. can hot enchilada sauce
8-oz. can tomato sauce
1 T. dried, minced onion

1-1/2 c. shredded American
   cheese, divided
2 c. tortilla chips, coarsely
   crushed and divided
1 c. sour cream

In a large skillet over medium heat, brown meat; drain. Stir in beans, sauces, onion and one cup cheese; mix well. Stir in one cup crushed tortilla chips. Transfer to a greased 1-1/2 quart casserole dish. Cover and bake at 375 degrees for 30 minutes. Sprinkle remaining chips around edge of casserole. Spoon sour cream evenly over top; sprinkle with remaining cheese. Bake, uncovered, until cheese melts, about 2 to 3 minutes. Serves 6.

Set a Lazy Susan on the dinner table. So handy for everyone to reach the sauces, condiments and toppings they like...just give it a spin!

Texas Taco Biscuit Bake

Rachel Phillips
New Castle, DE

I love all things taco...I also love casserole meals! This quick, tasty dish satisfies both of these loves at once. Adapt it easily to your family's taste by adding diced green chiles, Mexican-blend cheese or whatever else you like.

1 onion, chopped
2 T. oil
2-1/2 lbs. ground turkey
2 8-oz. cans tomato sauce
6-oz. can tomato paste
1/2 c. salsa
1-1/2 t. Italian seasoning
3/4 t. dried oregano

1 to 2 t. salt
1 c. frozen corn, thawed
1/2 c. diced tomatoes, drained
1-1/2 c. shredded Cheddar
  cheese, divided
10-oz. tube refrigerated
  buttermilk biscuits

In a large skillet over medium-low heat, cook onion in oil until tender. Add turkey and cook until no longer pink; drain. Add tomato sauce, tomato paste, salsa and seasonings. Cook and stir for 10 to 12 minutes, until heated through. Stir in corn, tomatoes and 3/4 cup cheese. Spoon turkey mixture into an ungreased 2-1/2 quart casserole dish; top with remaining cheese. Separate biscuits; arrange around edge of casserole dish on top of turkey mixture. Bake, uncovered, at 350 degrees for 20 to 25 minutes, until biscuits are golden and turkey mixture is hot and bubbly. Makes 6 to 10 servings.

"Fried" ice cream is a fun & festive ending to a Mexican meal. Roll scoops of vanilla ice cream in crushed frosted corn flake cereal and a sprinkle of cinnamon, then tuck in the freezer. At serving time, garnish with honey and whipped topping...yum!

All-in-One Noodle Supper

Michelle Taggart
Parker, CO

*My mom started making this comforting one-pot meal when
I was a child and I still make it today.*

8-oz. pkg. wide egg noodles,
   uncooked
2 lbs. ground beef
1/2 c. onion, chopped
10-3/4 oz. can cream of
   mushroom soup

3/4 c. milk
8-oz. pkg. cream cheese, cubed
   and softened
15-3/4 oz. can corn, drained
1-1/2 t. salt
1/8 t. pepper

Cook noodles as package directs; drain and set aside. Meanwhile, in a
large skillet over medium heat, brown beef. Add onion and cook until
tender; drain. Blend in soup, milk and cream cheese; stir in cooked
noodles and remaining ingredients. Reduce heat to low. Simmer for
15 to 20 minutes, until heated through and cream cheese is melted.
Serves 6 to 8.

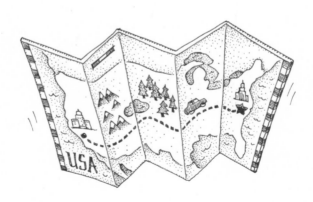

Old road maps make fun placemats...family members can share
memories of trips they've taken or daydream about places
they'd like to go. Simply cut maps to placemat size, then top
with postcards, ticket stubs or clippings and seal
in self-adhesive clear plastic.

My Mom's Stuffed Peppers

Nancy Girard
Chesapeake, VA

Mom made this quite often while I was growing up...it's now
one of my children's favorites too!

3 green peppers, halved and
   seeded
1 lb. lean ground beef
10-3/4 oz. can tomato soup
1/4 c. long-cooking rice,
   uncooked

1 T. sugar
1 T. dried, minced onion
8-oz. can tomato sauce

Arrange pepper halves in an ungreased 13"x9" baking pan. In a bowl,
mix together remaining ingredients except tomato sauce. Stuff peppers
evenly with beef mixture. Spoon tomato sauce over peppers. Cover
with aluminum foil. Bake at 350 degrees for one hour, or until peppers
are tender and beef is cooked through. Serves 3 to 4.

If it's been too long since you've visited with good friends,
why not host a casual get-together? Potlucks are so easy
to plan...everyone brings along their favorite dish to share.
It's all about food, fun and fellowship!

Forgotten Chicken & Rice

Susan Lovelace
Gastonia, NC

One of my family's favorite recipes...a scrumptious fix & forget delight!

1-1/2 c. long-cooking rice,
  uncooked
2 10-3/4 oz. cans cream of
  chicken soup
2 c. water

6 boneless, skinless chicken
  breasts
salt and pepper to taste
1.35-oz. pkg. onion soup mix

Spread uncooked rice evenly in a greased 13"x9" baking pan. Blend soup and water. Spoon half of soup mixture over rice; let stand for 3 to 4 minutes. Arrange chicken over rice; set aside. Add salt and pepper to remaining soup mixture; spoon over chicken. Sprinkle with dry soup mix. Cover with aluminum foil. Bake at 350 degrees for 1-1/2 to 2 hours, until rice is tender and chicken juices run clear when pierced. Serves 6.

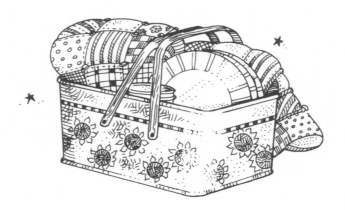

Savor a beautiful evening by carrying dinner to the backyard...invite the next-door neighbors too! Kids can work up an appetite before dinner playing hide & seek or tag. Top off the evening with a super-simple dessert like frozen fruit pops in warm weather or marshmallows toasted over a fire ring in cool weather.

Main *Dishes*

Busy-Day Chicken Paprikash

Bev Sajna
Rocky River, OH

When my kids come home from college, this dish is what they always want me to make. It's a real comfort food dinner!

4 to 5 chicken tenderloins
1 onion, sliced
1-1/2 c. water, divided
2-1/2 t. paprika
2 10-3/4 oz. cans cream of chicken soup

2 to 2-1/2 T. French onion sour cream dip
cooked egg noodles

In a large skillet over medium heat, sauté chicken and onion in one cup water, about 10 to 12 minutes. When chicken is almost done, remove it and cut into bite-size pieces. Return chicken to skillet and continue cooking until done, about 3 to 5 minutes. Mix in paprika. Stir in soup very well; add enough of remaining water to make a semi-thick consistency. Simmer for 5 minutes. Stir in dip until smooth. Simmer just until heated through; do not boil. Serve over cooked noodles. Serves 6.

Here's a simple way to add lots more flavor to noodles...just add a chicken or beef bouillon cube or two to the cooking water along with the noodles. It works with rice too!

Melinda's Veggie Stir-Fry

Melinda Daniels
Lewiston, ID

I really like stir-fries and chow mein, so I created this recipe using the items that I had in my garden and fridge. It is now one of my family's favorites and makes great leftovers too.

12-oz. pkg. spaghetti, uncooked
2 c. broccoli, cut into bite-size
   flowerets
1 c. snow pea pods, halved
2 stalks celery, thinly sliced

2 carrots, peeled and thinly
   sliced
1/2 onion, thinly sliced
1/4 green pepper, thinly sliced

Cook spaghetti as package directs; drain and set aside. Meanwhile, place vegetables into a steamer basket; place in a large stockpot filled with enough water to just reach the bottom of the basket. Heat over medium heat and steam for about 3 to 5 minutes, until just beginning to soften; drain. If crisper vegetables are desired, omit this step. When spaghetti and vegetables are done, add to Stir-Fry Sauce in skillet. Cook and stir over medium-high heat for about 15 minutes, to desired tenderness. Serves 6 to 8.

Stir-Fry Sauce:

3/4 c. olive oil
1/3 c. soy sauce
1/4 c. butter
2 T. Dijon mustard

2 T. sliced pepperoncini
2 cloves garlic, pressed
1 t. pepper

In a large skillet over low heat, mix all ingredients together. Simmer until heated through.

Shop for seasonal produce at farmers' markets and roadstands...corn and tomatoes in summer, acorn squash and pears in fall, cabbage and apples in winter and strawberries and asparagus in spring. Your family will dine on the freshest fruits & veggies year 'round.

Almond Chicken

Brooke Sottosanti
Brunswick, OH

*This was one of my favorite dinners that Mom made for us when
we were growing up. To this day, my brother still asks me
to make this for him when he comes to visit!*

1/3 c. soy sauce
1 t. garlic powder
3 lbs. boneless, skinless chicken
    breasts, cut into bite-size
    pieces
1/2 c. whole-wheat flour

1/2 c. almonds, finely chopped
1/2 t. salt
1/2 t. pepper
2 T. corn oil
cooked rice or lo mein noodles

Combine soy sauce and garlic powder in a large bowl; add chicken.
Let stand for about 20 minutes; drain. In a separate bowl, combine
flour, almonds, salt and pepper. Add chicken to flour mixture; toss to
coat lightly. Heat oil in a wok or large skillet over medium-high heat.
When oil is hot, add chicken mixture and reduce heat to medium.
Cover and cook, stirring often, for about 20 minutes, until chicken
juices run clear. Serve over cooked rice or noodles. Makes 8 servings.

If a casserole recipe serves too many for your family,
divide the ingredients into two smaller dishes, bake and
freeze one to enjoy later. It's a terrific way to have a
heat-and-eat meal ready to go when time is short.

Mexican Skillet Chicken & Twirls
Lori Comer
Kernersville, NC

*Our family really likes chicken, so when I found this recipe for
a one-pan meal, I decided to try it...yum!*

2 c. rotini pasta, uncooked	2 c. frozen corn
1 lb. boneless, skinless chicken	1/2 c. cream cheese, cubed
breasts	1/4 t. ground cumin
1 T. oil	1 c. finely shredded Mexican-
2 c. salsa	blend cheese, divided

Cook pasta as package directs; drain and set aside. Meanwhile, in a
large, deep non-stick skillet, cook chicken in oil until done, about
6 to 7 minutes. Add salsa, corn, cream cheese and cumin. Simmer for
about 5 minutes, stirring occasionally, until corn is heated through
and cream cheese is melted. Stir in cooked pasta and 1/2 cup shredded
cheese. Top with remaining cheese; cover and remove from heat. Let
stand for 5 minutes, or until cheese is melted. Serves 4.

Pick up a dozen pint-size Mason jars...they're fun and practical
for serving ice-cold lemonade, sweet tea or frosty root beer!

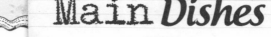

Family-Favorite Pork Tacos

Carol Lytle
Columbus, OH

My kids liked to order tacos just like these at our neighborhood Mexican restaurant, so I recreated the recipe to make at home. It's a great way to save money and such a hit, everyone in my family actually prefers them!

2 t. oil
1 lb. pork tenderloin, cubed
1 t. ground cumin
2 cloves garlic, minced
1 c. green or red salsa
Optional: 1/2 c. fresh cilantro, chopped

8 10-inch corn tortillas, warmed
Garnish: shredded lettuce, diced tomatoes, sliced avocado, sliced black olives, sour cream, shredded Cheddar cheese

Heat oil in a non-stick skillet over medium-high heat. Add pork cubes and cumin; cook until golden on all sides, about 5 minutes. Add garlic and cook for one minute; drain. Stir in salsa and heat through; stir in cilantro, if using. Using 2 forks, shred pork. Fill warmed tortillas with pork mixture; garnish as desired. Serves 4.

A speedy side for any south-of-the-border supper! Stir spicy salsa and shredded Mexican-blend cheese into hot cooked rice. Cover and let stand a few minutes, until the cheese melts.

Simple Shells & Chicken

Karen Skocik
Palos Heights, IL

My family requests this satisfying dish every week...and it's incredibly easy to make on short notice!

1-1/2 c. small shell macaroni, uncooked
10-3/4 oz. can cream of chicken soup
8-oz. container sour cream
3 to 4-lb. deli rotisserie chicken, cut into bite-size pieces
1 sleeve round buttery crackers, crushed
1/2 c. margarine, melted

Cook macaroni as package directs; drain and set aside. Meanwhile, mix together soup and sour cream in a large bowl. Add cooked macaroni and chicken; stir to combine. Transfer mixture to a 9"x9" baking pan sprayed with non-stick vegetable spray. Sprinkle crushed crackers evenly on top; drizzle with melted margarine. Bake, uncovered, at 350 degrees for 35 to 45 minutes. Serves 6 to 8.

Slow-Cooker Beer Chicken

Kristy Markners
Fort Mill, SC

This chicken is very moist and delicious. My three-year-old son gets so excited when we buy whole chickens at the grocery store...he says "Cock-a-doodle-zoo!" all through the store and on the way home!

3 to 4-lb. chicken
1/4 c. barbecue seasoning
12-oz. bottle regular or non-alcoholic beer

Spray a slow cooker with non-stick vegetable spray. Carefully loosen the chicken's skin. Rub seasoning generously under chicken skin and on top of skin. Place chicken in slow cooker; pour beer over chicken. Cover and cook on low setting for 8 hours. Serves 6.

Tom's Easy Meatloaf

Kelly Hargis
Essex, MD

This is my husband Tom's recipe. When we were first dating fifteen years ago, he made meatloaf for myself and my two young daughters, Erica and Bonnie. They both loved it and I did too...I was surprised that he could even cook! It's still a favorite at our house.

2 to 3 lbs. ground beef
2 10-3/4 oz. cans French onion
   soup

6-oz. pkg. stuffing mix
2 eggs, beaten

In a large bowl, mix together all ingredients well. Form into a loaf; place in a lightly greased 13"x9" baking pan. Bake, uncovered, at 350 degrees for 1-1/2 hours. Makes 6 to 8 servings.

If a tried & true meatloaf recipe is too large for your small family,
make meatloaf muffins instead! Fill greased muffin cups
and bake for 20 to 25 minutes at 350 degrees. Enjoy
some now...freeze the rest for later.

Mom's Beef Sopapillas

Anne Ptacnik
Yuma, CO

My mom has been making these mouthwatering sopapillas for as long as I can remember. They come out piping-hot and filled with cheesy goodness. Serve on a bed of lettuce...scrumptious!

2 c. all-purpose flour
1 t. baking powder
1 t. salt
1 T. shortening or oil
3/4 c. cold water
1/2 lb. ground beef, browned
   and drained

salt and pepper to taste
6 slices American cheese
oil for frying
Garnish: sour cream, salsa,
   sliced black olives, other
   favorite toppings

Mix flour, baking powder and salt together. In a separate bowl, combine shortening or oil and water; add to flour mixture and stir well. Form dough into 6 balls. Roll each ball into a very thin circle. Spoon about 1/4 cup beef onto the bottom half of each dough circle, leaving 1/2-inch edge of circle without filling. Sprinkle with salt and pepper; top with a cheese slice. Fold top half of dough over the cheese; crimp edges to seal dough around filling. In a Dutch oven over medium-high heat, heat oil to 375 degrees. Fry sopapillas until puffed and golden. Serve hot with desired toppings. Serves 6.

Make family mealtimes extra special! Even when you don't have guests coming for dinner, pull out the good china, set a vase of flowers on the table and light some candles. It's a terrific time to encourage children's good table manners...and make memories together too.

Tasty Tortilla Stack Pie

Connie Lufriu
Brandon, FL

*My children ask for this often! I made it up one night
when I was running low on groceries.*

1 lb. ground beef
10-3/4 oz. can Cheddar cheese
   soup
1 t. chili powder

1 t. taco seasoning mix
3 to 4 6-inch flour tortillas
1/2 c. shredded Cheddar cheese
Garnish: sour cream, salsa

Brown beef in a skillet over medium heat. Drain; stir in soup and
seasonings. Place one tortilla in the bottom of an ungreased 9" round
springform pan. Spoon 1/3 of beef mixture on top and sprinkle with a
little cheese. Repeat layers, ending with cheese on top. Cover with
aluminum foil. Bake at 350 degrees for about 20 minutes, until
heated through and cheese is melted. To serve, cut into wedges;
garnish as desired. Serves 4 to 5.

Take it easy and have a leftovers night once a week. Set out
yummy leftovers so everyone can choose their favorite. End with
cookies for dessert...what could be simpler?

Creamy Fettuccine Alfredo

Sheila Bane
Waynetown, IN

This has been one of my tried & true recipes for over twenty years.
It's a favorite of my kids...try it and you'll agree!

16-oz. pkg. fettuccine pasta,
  uncooked
1 t. salt
2/3 c. butter, softened
1-1/2 c. half-and-half, room
  temperature, divided

1-1/2 c. shredded Parmesan
  cheese
1/4 t. garlic salt
Garnish: additional shredded
  Parmesan cheese

Cook pasta as package directs, adding salt to cooking water. Remove pan from heat; drain pasta and return to pan. Add butter to warm pasta and mix well. Add 3/4 cup half-and-half to pasta; mix well. In a small bowl, mix together cheese and garlic salt. Add half of cheese mixture, remaining half-and-half and remaining cheese mixture to pasta mixture, stirring well after each addition. Garnish with additional cheese and serve immediately. Makes 6 servings.

Celebrate family birthdays, good report cards and other milestones with a special dinner plate for the person being honored! Look for a plate that says "You Are Special," create one yourself using glass & china paint or simply choose a brightly colored thrift-shop find that stands out from the rest of your dinnerware.

Desserts

Easy Pistachio Cake

Sharon Dennison
Floyds Knobs, IN

My mom has been making this great-tasting cake for years. It's so easy to bake & take to parties too, right in its pan.

18-1/2 oz. pkg. yellow or white
   cake mix
1/2 c. milk
1/2 c. water
1/2 c. oil

5 eggs, beaten
2 3.4-oz. pkgs. instant
   pistachio pudding mix
Optional: 1/2 c. chopped nuts

In a large bowl, blend together dry cake mix, milk, water, oil and eggs until smooth. Add dry pudding mix; stir well. Mix in nuts, if using. Pour batter into a lightly greased 13"x9" baking pan. Bake at 325 degrees for 45 minutes. Check for doneness with a toothpick; bake an additional 5 to 10 minutes, if needed. Cool completely; spread Cream Cheese Icing over cooled cake. Serves 12 to 15.

Cream Cheese Icing:

8-oz. pkg. cream cheese,
   softened
1/4 c. butter, softened
1 t. vanilla extract

16-oz. pkg. powdered sugar
3 to 4 T. milk
1 to 2 drops green food coloring
3/4 c. chopped nuts

In a large bowl, blend cream cheese, butter, vanilla and powdered sugar. Add enough milk for a spreadable consistency; stir in food coloring and nuts.

For the tastiest results, reduce your oven temperature by 25 degrees if you're using glass or dark baking pans...they retain heat more than shiny pans do.

Italian Love Cake

Amy Leona
Hightstown, NJ

This is a recipe from my wonderful mother. Its name is very fitting because she always showered her children with a lot of love! She baked this cake for many special occasions.

18-1/4 oz. pkg. marble cake mix
32-oz. container ricotta cheese
4 eggs, beaten
3/4 c. sugar
1 T. vanilla extract

1 c. milk
3.4-oz. pkg. instant vanilla
  pudding mix
8-oz. container frozen whipped
  topping, thawed

Prepare cake mix according to package directions. Pour batter into a greased and floured 13"x9" baking pan; set aside. In a large bowl, mix together ricotta cheese, eggs, sugar and vanilla. Carefully pour mixture over cake batter; do not stir. Bake at 350 degrees for 70 minutes. Cool cake completely in pan. In a bowl, whisk together milk and dry pudding mix; fold in whipped topping. Spread over cooled cake. Refrigerate until serving time. Serves 12.

A time-saving dessert...in parfait glasses, layer cherry pie filling with cubes of pound cake and creamy whipped topping. Top off servings with a sprinkle of cinnamon...yum!

Ladyfingers Icebox Cake

Caroline Schiller
Bayport, NY

This cake was one of my mother's favorites. My husband always requests it as his birthday cake.

18 to 24 ladyfingers, split and divided
2 1-oz. sqs. unsweetened baking chocolate
1/2 c. sugar
1/4 c. water
4 pasteurized eggs, separated
1 c. butter, softened
2-1/4 c. powdered sugar
1/2 t. vanilla extract
Garnish: whipped cream, chopped nuts

Line the bottom and sides of an ungreased 9" round springform pan with split ladyfingers, trimming off the bottoms to make ladyfingers stand. Set aside. In a double boiler over medium heat, cook and stir chocolate, sugar and water until chocolate is melted and smooth. In a separate bowl, beat egg yolks and gradually add to chocolate mixture, stirring constantly until smooth. Cool. Blend together butter, powdered sugar and vanilla; mix well. Add chocolate mixture; stir well and set aside. With an electric mixer on high speed, beat egg whites until stiff peaks form; fold into chocolate mixture. Spoon mixture into lined pan. Arrange any remaining ladyfingers on top. Garnish with whipped cream and chopped nuts. Refrigerate until serving time. To serve, remove outer ring of springform pan. Makes 12 servings.

Need a special tablecloth for a dessert buffet? There are so many charming print fabrics in many colors available at the craft store. Two to three yards is all you'll need. No hemming required...just trim the edges with pinking shears!

Banana Split Ice Cream

Charlotte Madison
Ellisville, MS

My mom made this ice cream for us one day and we all loved it.
Now I make it for our church ice cream socials, and there is
never any left...it tastes wonderful!

4.6-oz. pkg. cook & serve
   vanilla pudding mix
1 gal. milk, divided
2 14-oz. cans sweetened
   condensed milk
10-oz. jar maraschino cherries,
   drained and chopped

3 bananas, diced
1 c. chopped pecans
Optional: 1 c. sweetened flaked
   coconut

In a medium bowl, prepare pudding mix according to package
directions, using 3 cups of the milk. In a large bowl, combine
remaining milk with remaining ingredients. Add pudding mixture
and stir well. Pour into an ice cream freezer; freeze according to
manufacturer's directions. Makes 30 to 35 servings.

Be sure to save the red juice from jars of maraschino cherries.
Stir a little of it into lemonade, ginger ale or milk for
a sweet pink drink that kids will love.

Perfect Pecan Pie

Rogene Rogers
Bemidji, MN

This was my mother's recipe...it always brings smiles when it is served! Dollop with whipped cream for a luscious treat.

1/3 c. butter, softened
2/3 c. brown sugar, packed
3 eggs, beaten
1 c. light corn syrup

1 t. vanilla extract
1/4 t. salt
1 c. pecan halves
9-inch pie crust

Beat together butter, brown sugar and eggs. Add corn syrup, vanilla and salt; mix well. Stir in pecans; pour into unbaked crust. Bake at 350 degrees for 50 to 60 minutes, until set. Cool completely before cutting into wedges. Serves 8.

Tried & True Pie Dough

Sadie Phelan
Connellsville, PA

My mother always made 13 to 15 pies for the holidays using this recipe! It's the best...the dough is very easy to work with.

3-1/2 c. all-purpose flour
2 c. shortening
1 T. sugar

1 egg, beaten
1/2 c. cold water
1 T. vinegar

In a large bowl, blend together flour, shortening and sugar. In a separate bowl, beat together remaining ingredients. Add egg mixture to flour mixture; blend together. Divide into 3 balls; roll each out on a lightly floured surface. Makes 3 pie crusts.

Toting a pie to a picnic or party? A bamboo steamer from an import store is just the thing...it can even hold two pies at once.

Strawberry-Apple Pie

Mary Patenaude
Griswold, CT

*Deliciously different, this juicy pie makes a great dessert
for any time of year.*

3-1/2 c. apples, cored, peeled
and thinly sliced
1-1/4 c. strawberries, hulled
and sliced
1 T. lemon juice

1/4 c. all-purpose flour
1/2 c. plus 1/2 t. sugar, divided
2 9-inch pie crusts
1/8 t. cinnamon

Combine apples and strawberries in a bowl; drizzle with lemon juice.
In a separate bowl, combine flour and 1/2 cup sugar; sprinkle over
fruit mixture and toss lightly. Line a 9" pie plate with one pie crust;
spoon in fruit mixture. Top with remaining crust; trim, seal and flute
edges. Cut slits in top crust. Combine remaining sugar and cinnamon;
sprinkle over crust. Cover edges loosely with aluminum foil. Bake at
450 degrees for 10 minutes. Remove foil; reduce heat to 350 degrees
and bake an additional 35 to 40 minutes. Serves 6 to 8.

Before adding the top crust to a pie, cut out vents with a mini
cookie cutter...little hearts and stars leave the prettiest patterns!

Yellow Layer Cake

Vickie

*With three golden layers, this yummy made-from-scratch cake
is sure to be a hit at any party!*

4 eggs, separated
2-7/8 c. all-purpose flour
1-1/2 t. baking powder
1/2 t. salt
1 c. butter, softened

2 c. sugar
2 t. vanilla extract
1 c. milk
Garnish: favorite frosting

With an electric mixer on high speed, beat egg whites in a small bowl
until stiff peaks form. In a medium bowl, combine flour, baking
powder and salt. In a large bowl, beat butter on medium speed of
electric mixer; gradually beat in sugar until fluffy. Beat in egg yolks,
one at a time, and vanilla. With a wooden spoon, stir flour mixture
into butter mixture by thirds, alternating with milk. Fold in egg
whites. Divide batter among 3 greased and floured 9" round cake
pans. Bake at 350 degrees for 35 minutes, until a toothpick tests
clean. Cool; assemble with frosting. Serves 12.

Merry Mocha Frosting

*Susann Minall-Hunter
Spring Hill, FL*

*Once when I was ten, Mom baked her best chocolate cake for a picnic.
When I got home from school, I saw the bowl of frosting on the counter.
I stuck in my finger to take a taste...before I knew it, the bowl was
empty! Mom didn't get mad...but from then on, she always hid the
frosting bowl!*

1/2 c. butter, softened
1 pasteurized egg yolk
2 T. strong brewed coffee

2 1-oz. sqs. baking chocolate,
  melted
2-1/2 c. powdered sugar

Beat together butter and egg yolk in a small bowl. Add coffee and
melted chocolate; mix well. Gradually add powdered sugar; beat until
smooth. Makes about 3-1/2 cups, enough for 2, 8-inch cakes.

Surprise Butter Cake

Rebecca Ludman
Gilbertsville, PA

Years ago, a very dear cousin of my husband was talking about the wonderful bakery butter cakes he enjoyed when he was growing up in Philadelphia in the 1950s. Now I surprise him with this cake on special occasions. My children are extremely close to this cousin and it makes the surprise even more special.

18-1/2 oz. pkg. yellow cake mix
1/2 c. butter, melted and slightly
   cooled
4 eggs

8-oz. pkg. cream cheese,
   softened
16-oz. pkg. powdered sugar
1 t. vanilla extract

In a large bowl, combine dry cake mix, butter and 2 eggs. Blend well to make a very thick batter. Pat into the bottom of a greased 13"x9" baking pan; set aside. Beat together remaining ingredients; pour over batter. Bake at 350 degrees for 30 to 35 minutes; do not overbake. Topping will look runny, but will set as it cools. Makes 18 to 24 servings.

Create a charming cake stand with thrift-store finds. Attach a glass plate with epoxy glue to a short glass vase or candle stand for a base. Let dry completely before using...so clever!

Best-Ever Strawberry Shortcake

Emma Johnson
Lithopolis, OH

My mom always made this shortcake when our strawberries ripened in early June. She received this recipe from her mother and it has always been a family favorite. In fact, this dessert is so good it has even been featured at my brother-in-law's fine-dining restaurant!

1/2 c. butter, softened
1 c. sugar
2 eggs, beaten
1 t. vanilla extract
1/2 c. milk

2 c. all-purpose flour
1 T. baking powder
1/4 t. salt
Garnish: sliced strawberries,
  whipped cream

In a bowl, combine butter and sugar. Beat with an electric mixer on medium speed until smooth; beat in eggs, vanilla and milk. In a separate bowl, mix flour, baking powder and salt. Gradually add flour mixture to butter mixture; mix well. Spoon batter into a greased 9"x9" baking pan. Bake at 350 degrees for 40 to 50 minutes, until a toothpick inserted near the center tests clean. Cut shortcake into squares; top with strawberries and whipped cream. Makes 9 servings.

Fresh-picked berries are a special country pleasure. Store them in a colander in the refrigerator to let cold air circulate around them. Wash them when you're ready to use them.

Scrumptious Strawberry Torte

Jan Nickell
Mount Zion, IL

This is my tried & true recipe for family get-togethers and carry-ins at work...it's an easy make-ahead and oh-so good! In the summertime, you can use sliced fresh strawberries.

2 3.4-oz. pkgs. instant vanilla pudding mix
2 c. milk
8-oz. container frozen whipped topping, thawed
1 angel food cake, cubed

2 6-oz. pkgs. strawberry gelatin mix
2-1/2 c. boiling water
2 10-oz. pkgs. frozen strawberries, thawed and drained

In a large bowl, whisk together dry pudding mix and milk. Fold in whipped topping and cake cubes. Spread mixture in a 13"x9" glass baking pan; cover and chill for an hour. In a separate bowl, combine dry gelatin mix and boiling water. Stir to dissolve; fold in strawberries. Cover and chill until slightly thickened, 45 to 55 minutes. Gently pour gelatin mixture over cake mixture. Cover and chill until set, about 2 to 3 hours. Makes 10 to 12 servings.

Top off your best desserts with freshly whipped cream...it isn't hard to make. With an electric mixer on high speed, beat one cup heavy cream until soft peaks form. Add one tablespoon sugar and one teaspoon vanilla extract, then continue to beat until stiff peaks form. Luscious!

Hot Cinnamon Pudding

Jennie Wiseman
Coshocton, OH

I used to make this cozy pudding for my girls when they were little.
They would sled down a tiny hill in front of our home with their dad.
When they came back in, they warmed up with this pudding.

2 c. brown sugar, packed
1-1/2 c. cold water
1/4 c. butter, melted and divided
3/4 c. sugar
1 c. milk
2 c. all-purpose flour

2 t. baking powder
2 t. cinnamon
1/4 t. salt
Optional: chopped nuts
Garnish: whipped cream or
    vanilla ice cream

Mix together brown sugar, water and 2 tablespoons butter. Pour into
a greased and floured 1-1/2 quart casserole dish. In a bowl, mix
together remaining ingredients except nuts and garnish. Pour over
brown sugar mixture. Top with nuts, if desired. Bake at 350 degrees
for 45 minutes. Garnish as desired; serve warm. Serves 6.

English Bread Pudding

Karen Foster
Hampshire, England

This recipe is made with leftover bread. It was handed down to me
from my mum and everybody loves it!

10 slices day-old bread, torn
1/2 c. shortening
1/2 c. sugar
1-1/2 c. golden raisins

apple pie spice to taste
Optional: custard or whipping
    cream

Place bread in a large bowl. Cover with cold water; let stand for
30 minutes. Drain; squeeze water from bread and return to bowl.
Add shortening and sugar; mix well. Add raisins and spice; mix
thoroughly. Place in a lightly greased 2-quart casserole dish. Bake at
350 degrees for one hour. Serve warm or cold, garnished as desired.
Makes 8 to 10 servings.

Grandmother's Goofy Cake

Cathie Ellison
Ontario, Canada

This chocolate cake recipe came from my grandmother to my mum to me. I believe it came about during the First World War when certain ingredients were hard to get. Birthday and holiday celebrations are just not complete without Goofy Cake for dessert. No other dessert is suitable, as far as my family is concerned!

1-1/2 c. all-purpose flour	1 c. hot water
1 c. sugar	5 T. butter, melted
1/4 c. baking cocoa	1 T. white vinegar
1 t. baking powder	1 t. vanilla extract
1 t. baking soda	Garnish: favorite frosting
1/2 t. salt	Optional: vanilla ice cream
1 t. instant coffee granules	

Preheat oven to 400 degrees. In a large bowl, sift together flour, sugar, cocoa, baking powder, baking soda and salt; set aside. Dissolve coffee granules in hot water; add to flour mixture. Add butter, vinegar and vanilla; stir until well blended. Pour into a greased 8"x8" baking pan. Place pan into preheated oven, then reduce heat to 350 degrees. Bake for 35 to 45 minutes. Frost when cooled. Serve with ice cream, if desired. Serves 9.

Grease and flour cake pans in one easy step! Combine 1/2 cup shortening with 1/4 cup all-purpose flour. Keep this handy mix in a covered jar stored at room temperature.

People-Pleasin' Peach Pie

Kay Marone
Des Moines, IA

*A positively perfect peach pie my mom taught me how to make,
for when the sun is shining and the peaches are ripe.*

2 9-inch pie crusts
5 c. peaches, pitted, peeled and
   sliced
2 t. lemon juice
1/2 t. vanilla extract
1 c. sugar

1/4 c. cornstarch
1/2 t. cinnamon
1/4 t. nutmeg
1/8 t. salt
2 T. butter, sliced
1 to 2 T. milk

Line a 9" pie plate with one crust and set aside. In a large bowl,
combine peaches, lemon juice and vanilla. In a separate bowl, mix
sugar, cornstarch, spices and salt. Add sugar mixture to peach
mixture; toss gently to coat. Spoon into pie crust; dot with butter.
With a small cookie cutter, cut vents in remaining crust, reserving
cut-outs. Place crust on top of pie; trim and seal edges. Brush milk
over top crust and cut-outs; arrange cut-outs on crust. Cover edges
loosely with aluminum foil. Bake at 400 degrees for 40 minutes.
Remove foil and bake an additional 10 to 15 minutes, until crust is
golden and filling is bubbly. Makes 6 to 8 servings.

A mother is a person who seeing there are only four pieces of pie
for five people, promptly announces she never did care for pie.

-Tenneva Jordan

Desserts

Chocolate Chess Pie

Cherylann Smith
Efland, NC

*This simple, yummy old-fashioned recipe was given to me by
my Mama Chris, who received it from her grandma.*

1/4 c. baking cocoa
1/2 c. butter
1/4 c. milk
1-1/2 c. sugar

3 eggs, beaten
1 t. vanilla extract
1/8 t. salt
9-inch deep-dish pie crust

In a saucepan over low heat, combine cocoa, butter and milk. Stir
until smooth. Remove from heat; cool slightly. Add sugar, eggs,
vanilla and salt; beat well. Pour cocoa mixture into crust. Bake at
350 degrees for 45 minutes, or until set. Cool before slicing. Serves 8.

Sweet vintage pie plates can easily be found at tag sales and flea
markets...maybe even in Mom's cupboard! Words stamped inside
like..."Flaky Crust" or "Mellow Rich Pie" make them so charming.
They're just right for sharing a pie with a special friend.

Cherries in the Snow

Karen Van Den Berge
Holland, MI

When I was growing up, my mother would make this dessert for my siblings and me. We requested it often and were happy if there were leftovers...we would eat them for breakfast the next day!

1 c. all-purpose flour
1/2 c. margarine, softened
1/4 c. brown sugar, packed
1/2 c. chopped walnuts
8-oz. pkg. cream cheese, softened

2 c. powdered sugar
2 t. vanilla extract
8-oz. container frozen whipped topping, thawed
21-oz. can cherry pie filling

In a bowl, mix together flour, margarine, brown sugar and walnuts. Press into an ungreased 13"x9" baking pan. Bake at 375 degrees for 15 minutes. Remove from oven. Crumble baked crust in pan and pat down; cool completely. Blend together cream cheese, powdered sugar and vanilla; fold in whipped topping. Spoon mixture over cooled crust. Top with pie filling and serve. Makes 16 servings.

For a speedy dessert garnish, chop nuts and toast them in a shallow baking pan at 350 degrees for 5 to 10 minutes. Cool, then place in plastic bags and freeze...ready to sprinkle on pies, cakes or ice cream whenever you want them.

Snowy Glazed Apple Squares

Janet Seabern
Winona, MN

My mother used to make this dessert when I was a young girl. I still make it for parties and church luncheons when apples are in season.

2-1/2 c. all-purpose flour
1/2 t. salt
1 c. shortening
2 eggs, separated
1/2 to 2/3 c. milk
1-1/2 c. corn flake cereal,
    crushed

8 baking apples, peeled, cored
    and sliced
1 c. sugar
1 t. cinnamon

In a bowl, mix flour and salt; cut in shortening. Beat egg yolks in a measuring cup; add enough milk to measure 2/3 cup. Add to flour mixture and mix lightly. Divide dough into 2 parts, one slightly larger than the other. Roll out larger portion into a 15-inch by 10-inch rectangle. Place on a lightly greased 15"x10" jelly-roll pan. Sprinkle evenly with cereal; arrange apple slices over cereal. Mix sugar and cinnamon; sprinkle over apples. Roll out remaining dough and place on top; seal edges and cut slits in top. Beat egg whites until foamy and spread over dough. Bake at 350 degrees for one hour. Cool slightly; spread with Vanilla Glaze. Cut into squares. Makes about 2-1/2 dozen.

Vanilla Glaze:

1-1/2 c. powdered sugar
3 T. water

1/2 t. vanilla extract

Stir together until smooth.

Use a sugar shaker to save clean-up time in the kitchen...it's ideal for dusting powdered sugar onto cookies and desserts warm from the oven.

Slow-Cooker Tapioca Pudding

Leisha Howard
Seattle, WA

When I was a child, my mom and I often made stovetop tapioca pudding and I was the stirrer. Even though both my arms would get tired, I loved helping her in the kitchen. Now that I'm older, I've mastered this slow-cooker recipe...it's just as yummy!

8 c. milk
1 c. small pearl tapioca,
   uncooked
1 to 1-1/2 c. sugar
4 eggs, beaten

1 t. vanilla extract
1/2 t. almond extract
Garnish: whipped cream, sliced
   fresh fruit

Add milk, tapioca and sugar to a slow cooker; stir gently. Cover and cook on high setting for 3 hours. In a bowl, mix together eggs, extracts and 2 spoonfuls of hot milk mixture from slow cooker. Slowly stir mixture into slow cooker. Cover and cook on high setting for an additional 20 minutes. Chill overnight. Garnish as desired. Serves 10 to 12.

Bragging-Rights Banana Pudding

Mary Jackson
Fishers, IN

This recipe was handed down from my wonderful mother-in-law.
It is a definite crowd-pleaser!

5-1/4 oz. pkg. instant vanilla
   pudding mix
3 c. milk
16-oz. container sour cream
12-oz. container frozen whipped
   topping, thawed

10-oz. pkg. vanilla wafers,
   divided
4 bananas, sliced and divided

In a bowl, with an electric mixer on low speed, beat dry pudding mix and milk for 2 to 3 minutes, until thickened. Beat in sour cream; fold in topping. Set aside several vanilla wafers. In a large deep bowl, layer half each of remaining wafers, bananas and pudding mixture. Repeat layering. Crush reserved wafers and sprinkle on top. Cover; chill until served. Serves 10 to 15.

Pineapple-Cherry Spoon Cake

Phyllis Peters
Three Rivers, MI

This is so simple...great for busy moms! It's easy to keep the ingredients on hand for whipping up a quick dessert for guests.

20-oz. can crushed pineapple,
   drained
21-oz. can cherry pie filling

18-1/2 oz. pkg. yellow cake mix
3/4 c. butter, melted

Spread pineapple in a lightly greased 13"x9" baking pan. Top with pie filling and sprinkle with dry cake mix. Drizzle butter evenly over cake mix. Bake at 350 degrees for 35 to 40 minutes. Serves 8 to 10.

Make a delightful sauce in a jiffy to spoon over ice cream
or slices of pound cake. Purée strawberry or apricot preserves
with a few tablespoons of fruit juice...yummy!

Moist Chocolate Cake

Suzanne Ruminski
Johnson City, NY

I got this recipe from my mother, who got it from her mother, who we believe got it from her mother! Now I'm sharing it with my own soon-to-be-married daughter. It has been baked for many family birthdays and shared with co-workers too...everyone who tries this cake requests the recipe!

2 c. sugar
1/2 c. shortening
2 eggs, beaten
2 c. all-purpose flour
1 t. salt
1 t. baking powder

1 T. baking soda
2/3 c. baking cocoa
2 c. boiling water
1 t. vanilla extract
Garnish: favorite frosting
Optional: shredded coconut

In a large bowl, blend together sugar, shortening and eggs. Add flour, salt, baking powder and baking soda; beat well. Add cocoa, water and vanilla; pour into a greased 13"x9" baking pan. Bake at 350 degrees for 25 to 30 minutes, until cake tests done. Cool; garnish as desired. Serves 8 to 10.

Coconutty Pecan Frosting

Sarah Mae Emack
Hildale, UT

Scrumptious...perfect for topping a German chocolate cake.

1 c. evaporated milk
1 c. agave syrup or sugar
3 egg yolks
1/2 c. butter

1 t. vanilla extract
2 c. sweetened flaked coconut
1-1/2 c. chopped pecans

In a saucepan over medium-low heat, combine all ingredients except coconut and pecans. Cook for about 12 minutes until thickened, stirring constantly. Remove from heat. Stir in coconut and pecans; beat until cool. Makes about 6 cups frosting.

Hot Milk Cake

Karen Dean
New Market, MD

My mom used to bake this delightful made-from-scratch cake for our family. The chocolate frosting makes it extra special!

4 eggs, beaten
2 c. sugar
2 c. all-purpose flour
2 t. baking powder

1/4 t. salt
1 t. vanilla extract
1/2 c. butter
1 c. milk

In a large bowl, beat together eggs and sugar. Add flour, baking powder, salt and vanilla; mix well and set aside. In a saucepan over medium heat, combine butter and milk. Bring to a boil; cool slightly and add to batter. Mix well. Pour batter into a greased and floured 13"x9" baking pan. Bake at 350 degrees for 30 minutes, until cake tests done. Cool; frost with Bitter Chocolate Frosting. Makes 20 to 25 servings.

Bitter Chocolate Frosting:

5 1-oz. sqs. unsweetened
   baking chocolate
1 T. butter, softened
1 t. vanilla extract

1-1/2 to 1-3/4 c. powdered
   sugar
3 to 5 T. whipping cream

Melt chocolate in a double boiler over medium heat. Remove from heat; gradually stir in butter and vanilla. With an electric mixer on low speed, beat in powdered sugar and cream to desired consistency.

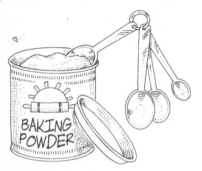

Not sure if your baking powder is still good? Try this simple test: stir one teaspoon baking powder into 1/2 cup hot water. If it fizzes, go ahead and use it.

Big Yellow Sheet Cake

Claire Boucher
Ocean Springs, MS

A terrific cake for large family get-togethers and potlucks!

18-1/2 oz. pkg. yellow cake
   mix, divided
4 eggs, divided
1/2 c. margarine, softened
1-1/2 c. water

1/2 c. brown sugar, packed
1-1/2 c. corn syrup
Optional: chopped nuts
Garnish: favorite frosting

In a large bowl, mix together 1-2/3 cups dry cake mix, one egg, margarine and water. Pour into a greased 13"x9" baking pan. Bake at 325 degrees for 15 minutes. Mix together remaining cake mix, remaining eggs, brown sugar, corn syrup and nuts, if using. Pour into center of partially baked cake. Return to oven; bake at 325 degrees for about one hour. Cool; frost as desired. Serves 12 to 15.

Best-Ever Bakery Frosting

Renee Shock
Beaver Dams, NY

We love the taste of this frosting! A lady in Nunda, New York gave me this recipe when we stopped in her little bakery, many years ago.

2 16-oz. pkgs. powdered sugar
1 c. shortening

1 t. clear vanilla extract
1/2 to 3/4 c. milk

In a large bowl, mix all ingredients together just until moistened, adding milk as needed. Do not overbeat. Makes about 3 cups, enough to frost 6 dozen cookies or 2 large cakes.

When frosting a layer cake, tuck strips of wax paper under
the edges of the bottom layer. Remove them after the cake is frosted
for a neat and tidy cake plate with no frosting smudges.

Desserts

Deborah's Blueberry Cake

Deborah Goodrich
Smithfield, VA

All my friends call me "Betty Crocker" because I love to cook and share. Whenever I bake this blueberry cake, they all make sure to get a slice of it!

1 c. butter, softened
2 c. sugar
4 eggs, room temperature
1 t. vanilla extract
3 c. all-purpose flour

1 t. baking powder
1/2 t. salt
2 c. blueberries
Garnish: raw or coarse sugar

In a large bowl, beat together butter and sugar. Add eggs, one at a time, beating well after each addition. Beat until fluffy and add vanilla. In a separate bowl, mix together flour, baking powder and salt. Set aside one cup of flour mixture. Add remaining flour mixture to butter mixture and beat well. Dredge berries in reserved flour mixture. Gently fold berry mixture into batter. Spoon into a greased and floured 10" tube pan. Sprinkle raw or coarse sugar on top. Bake at 350 degrees for 1-1/4 hours, or until a cake tester inserted near the center comes out clean. Cool and top with Lemony Glaze, if desired. Makes 24 servings.

Lemony Glaze:

1/2 c. powdered sugar
1/2 c. milk

1 t. lemon zest

Stir all ingredients together in a small bowl until smooth.

Freshly grated citrus zest adds so much flavor to recipes and it's easy to keep on hand. Whenever you use an orange, lemon or lime, just grate the peel first. Keep it frozen in an airtight container for up to two months.

Tiramisu Toffee Treat

Sharon Tillman
Hampton, VA

This recipe is a really yummy version of one that came from my great-grandmother. One Sunday a month I go home from college, and my grandmother, mother, sisters and I visit over mugs of coffee and squares of this creamy dessert.

10-3/4 oz. pkg. frozen pound
   cake, thawed and cut into
   9 slices
3/4 c. strong brewed coffee
1 c. sugar
1/2 c. chocolate syrup
8-oz. pkg. cream cheese,
   softened

2 c. whipping cream
2 1.4-oz. chocolate-covered
   toffee candy bars, chopped
Optional: whipped cream,
   chocolate syrup

Arrange cake slices in the bottom of an ungreased 11"x7" baking pan. Drizzle coffee over cake; set aside. In a large bowl, with an electric mixer on medium speed, beat sugar, chocolate syrup and cream cheese until smooth. Add whipping cream; beat on medium speed until light and fluffy. Spread over cake. Sprinkle cake with chopped candy. Cover and refrigerate for one to 8 hours. If desired, garnish portions at serving time with dollops of whipped cream and a drizzle of chocolate syrup. Makes 8 servings.

Make a handy potholder rack from a vintage wooden rolling pin. Place a row of cup hooks along one side and add a strip of homespun tied to each end for hanging. So simple!

Desserts

Dulce De Licious

Tiffany Brinkley
Broomfield, CO

If you're a busy mom like me, you'll appreciate this super-easy recipe. And it's as good as it sounds...this is the dessert my kids request for every special occasion. Someone's birthday? Dulce De Licious. Christmas? Dulce De...well, you get the idea!

40 vanilla wafers, divided
1-1/4 c. cold milk
2 3.4-oz. pkgs. instant white
   chocolate pudding mix

8-oz. container frozen whipped
   topping, thawed
1/4 c. caramel ice cream
   topping, divided

Chop 4 vanilla wafers; set aside. Line a 9"x5" loaf pan with aluminum foil, with ends of foil extending over sides of pan. Arrange 12 vanilla wafers in a single layer in bottom of pan; set aside. In a large bowl, whisk milk and pudding mix together for 2 minutes, until well blended. Gently stir in whipped topping. Spoon 1/3 of pudding mixture into pan; top with 12 vanilla wafers and 2 tablespoons caramel topping. Repeat layering with pudding mixture, vanilla wafers and topping. Cover with remaining pudding mixture. Sprinkle with reserved vanilla wafer crumbs; press gently into pudding mixture. Cover and freeze for 4 hours, until firm. Shortly before serving time, lift dessert from pan, using foil handles; peel off foil. Place on a serving plate; let stand for 15 minutes before slicing. Makes 10 to 12 servings.

Sparkly sugared fruit garnishes are simple to make and so pretty.
Simply brush strawberries or grapes with light corn syrup,
then roll in super-fine sugar.

Rich Oatmeal Cake

Babette Burgess
Battle Creek, MI

*Everyone enjoys this easy-to-make cake! A friend gave this recipe
to my mother, who made a few additions of her own.*

1-1/2 c. boiling water
1 c. quick-cooking oats,
   uncooked
1/2 c. butter
1 c. sugar
1 c. brown sugar, packed
2 eggs, beaten

1 t. vanilla extract
2 t. cinnamon
1/2 t. nutmeg
1-1/3 c. all-purpose flour
1 t. baking powder
1 t. baking soda
1/2 t. salt

In a medium bowl, pour boiling water over oats; let stand for
20 minutes. In a separate bowl, blend butter and sugars; add to oats.
Add eggs, vanilla and spices; beat well and set aside. In a small bowl,
mix together remaining ingredients. Add to oat mixture and stir well.
Pour into a greased 13"x9" baking pan. Bake at 350 degrees for 35 to
40 minutes, until cake tests done. Spread Coconut Topping evenly
over cake. Place under the broiler for about 10 minutes, until topping
is golden and bubbly. Serves about 12.

Coconut Topping:

1/4 c. plus 2 t. butter, melted
1 c. sugar
1/2 c. evaporated milk

1 t. vanilla extract
1/2 c. sweetened flaked coconut
Optional: 1/2 c. chopped nuts

Combine all ingredients and mix well.

208

Chocolate Chip-Oat Cookies

Tracey Ten Eyck
Austin, TX

This recipe was handed down to me by my mother, who is now ninety-five. Whenever we had a hankering for homemade cookies, this was the recipe we turned to. We still have the original recipe clipping, now tattered and torn...we think it came from a ladies' magazine, perhaps as far back as the 1940s.

1 c. shortening
3/4 c. brown sugar, packed
3/4 c. sugar
2 eggs
1 t. hot water
1-1/2 c. all-purpose flour
1 t. baking soda
1 t. salt

12-oz. pkg. semi-sweet
  chocolate chips
2 c. long-cooking oats,
  uncooked
Optional: 1 c. nuts, finely
  chopped
1 t. vanilla extract

In a large bowl, beat shortening until soft. Gradually add sugars, blending until light and fluffy. Add eggs, one at a time, beating well after each addition. Stir in hot water. In a separate bowl, mix together flour, baking soda and salt; gradually add flour mixture to shortening mixture. Stir in chocolate chips, oats and nuts, if desired; mix thoroughly. Add vanilla and blend well. Drop by 1/2 teaspoonfuls onto greased baking sheets. Bake at 375 degrees for 8 to 10 minutes, until tops are golden. Makes about 8 dozen.

Serve up warm, fresh-baked cookies at a moment's notice!
Roll your favorite cookie dough into balls and freeze them on
a tray, then pop them into a freezer bag. Later, just pull out the number
of cookies you need, thaw briefly and bake.

World's Best Pecan Cookies

Lisanne Miller
Canton, MS

This recipe is from Gladys Edwards, my good friend Margaret's mother. When we moved to Mississippi from Maine, Margaret shared her mother's recipe and her cookies...what a great welcome to the South! It makes a huge batch of crisp and delicious cookies.

1 c. margarine	4 c. all-purpose flour
1 c. oil	1 t. baking soda
1 c. sugar	1 t. salt
1 c. powdered sugar	1 t. cream of tartar
2 eggs, beaten	1 c. pecans, finely chopped
1 t. vanilla extract	

In a large bowl, blend together margarine, oil, sugars, eggs and vanilla. In a separate bowl, mix together remaining ingredients except pecans. Add flour mixture to margarine mixture; mix well. Stir in pecans. Cover and chill dough for at least one hour. Pinch off small balls of dough and place on greased baking sheets; flatten with a fork. Bake at 325 degrees for 10 to 12 minutes. If dough becomes too soft, return it to the refrigerator for at least 30 minutes. Makes about 8 dozen.

Welcome new neighbors with a basket of homemade cookies. Tuck in a map of the neighborhood with all of your favorite spots marked with shiny stars...sure to be much appreciated!

Desserts

Grandma Saint's Fridge Cookies

Mary Ann Saint
Indian Land, SC

My sister-in-law in Louisiana always made these cookies for us when we visited. She knew my husband would be so happy to eat the cookies his mother used to make. In fact, it made all of us happy...they're the most delicious refrigerator cookies I've ever tasted. You can't eat just one...they are addictive!

1 c. butter, softened
1/2 c. sugar
1/2 c. brown sugar, packed
1 egg, beaten
1 t. vanilla extract

2 c. all-purpose flour
1/2 t. baking soda
1/4 t. salt
1 c. chopped pecans

In a large bowl, blend butter and sugars. Add egg and vanilla; mix well. In a separate bowl, mix together remaining ingredients except pecans. Add flour mixture to butter mixture and stir well; add pecans. Divide dough into 2 parts. Form each part into a roll; wrap rolls in wax paper. Refrigerate at least 2 hours to overnight. Cut dough into 1/2-inch thick slices; arrange 2 inches apart on lightly greased baking sheets. Bake at 350 degrees for 14 to 15 minutes. Makes 4 dozen.

A nifty way to make perfectly shaped slice & bake cookies! Pack dough into clean, empty small orange juice cans and freeze. To bake, let thaw for 15 minutes, then remove bottom of can and push up dough. Slice dough across open end of can...ready to bake!

Ranger Cookies

Heather Plasterer
Colorado Springs, CO

The scrumptious taste of these crunchy cookies will always take me back home. Mom made them often while we were growing up and took them along to lots of get-togethers. Yum!

1 c. shortening
1 c. sugar
1 c. brown sugar, packed
2 eggs, beaten
1 t. vanilla extract
2 c. all-purpose flour
1 t. baking powder

1 t. baking soda
1/2 t. salt
2 c. long-cooking oats, uncooked
2 c. crispy rice cereal
1 c. sweetened flaked coconut

In a large bowl, blend together shortening and sugars; beat in eggs and vanilla. In a separate bowl, mix together flour, baking powder, baking soda and salt; stir in oats, cereal and coconut. Add flour mixture to shortening mixture; mix well. Drop by rounded teaspoonfuls onto ungreased baking sheets. Bake at 350 degrees for 10 minutes. Makes 2-1/2 dozen.

Show off a collection of favorite stoneware mixing bowls on open-front kitchen shelves. Add a shelf edging of scrapbooking paper, trimmed with decorative-edge scissors...so pretty!

Desserts

Pastel Bon-Bon Cookies

Sharon Demers
Dolores, CO

These cookies just melt in your mouth! My mother used to make them every spring. The pastel colors are beautiful and the delicate flavor of vanilla and almond is really special.

1 c. shortening
1-1/2 c. powdered sugar
1 egg, beaten
1/2 t. vanilla extract
1/2 t. almond extract

2-3/4 c. all-purpose flour
1/2 t. baking soda
1/2 t. cream of tartar
1/2 t. salt
few drops desired food colorings

In a large bowl, blend together shortening and powdered sugar. Add egg and extracts; beat well. In a separate bowl, mix together remaining ingredients except food coloring. Add to shortening mixture; beat well. Divide dough into 4 parts and place in separate bowls. Add one drop of food coloring of choice to each part and knead until color is evenly distributed. Cover; chill dough for one hour. Form dough into small balls the size of large marbles. Place on ungreased baking sheets. Flatten slightly with the bottom of a glass tumbler dipped in flour. Bake at 350 degrees for 10 to 15 minutes, watching carefully. To retain their pretty pastel colors, do not allow cookies to turn golden. Makes 4 dozen.

Invite all the little girls in the neighborhood to a tea party! Set a low table with a lacy tablecloth, a nosegay of sweet flowers and your prettiest teacups. Add a steamy pot of chamomile tea, little sandwiches cut in fancy shapes and a big platter of dainty cookies. Such fun!

Butterscotch-Chocolate Chip Cookies

*Tina Smith
Reidsville, GA*

My children come running when they smell these cookies! Every year during the fall and winter carnivals at school, the boys' teachers ask me to send these cookies. I also give batches of these away for gifts and everyone absolutely loves them. Be sure to follow this recipe exactly or the cookies will come out flat...but still tasty!

2-1/2 c. all-purpose flour
1-1/4 t. baking soda
1/2 t. salt
1 c. butter, softened
1 c. brown sugar, packed
3/4 c. sugar

2 eggs, beaten
1-1/2 t. vanilla extract
Optional: 1/2 t. almond extract
2/3 c. milk chocolate chips
2/3 c. butterscotch chips

In a bowl, mix together flour, baking soda and salt; set aside. In a separate bowl, with an electric mixer on medium speed, beat butter until it is light and clings to the bowl, about 30 to 45 seconds. Add sugars. Continue to beat on medium speed for 4 to 5 minutes, scraping bowl down 2 to 3 times. In a small bowl, whisk eggs and extracts together. Pour egg mixture into butter mixture very slowly; continue to beat for 4 to 5 minutes, until mixture is very fluffy and resembles whipped peanut butter. With beater on low speed, add flour mixture; mix well. Fold in chips; beat a few more seconds, just until chips are mixed in thoroughly. Do not overmix. Drop by tablespoonfuls onto lightly greased baking sheets. Bake at 400 degrees for 8 to 10 minutes, until edges are golden. Store in an airtight container. Makes about 4 dozen.

Wrap up Mom's big yellowware mixing bowl along with her prized cookie recipe for a child who's learning to bake...sure to be a cherished gift!

Desserts

Hays Cookies

Sherilyn Rank
Warsaw, IN

My mom first sampled these brown sugar cookie bars at a church carry-in dinner. She asked for the recipe and when she received it later, there was no name given for the cookies. Because Mrs. Hays was the lady who gave her the recipe, Mom dubbed these "Hays Cookies" and we've known them that way ever since!

1-1/2 c. all-purpose flour
1/2 c. butter
1/2 t. salt
1 c. brown sugar, packed and
   divided

2 eggs, beaten
1/2 c. sugar
1/4 c. chopped pecans or
   walnuts
Garnish: 1 T. powdered sugar

In a large bowl, mix together flour, butter, salt and 1/2 cup brown sugar. Press mixture into the bottom of a lightly greased 9"x9" baking pan; set aside. In a small bowl, mix together eggs, sugar and remaining brown sugar. Spoon over flour mixture in pan; sprinkle with nuts. Bake at 350 degrees for 30 minutes. Remove from oven; let stand for 10 minutes. Sprinkle with powdered sugar; cut into bars while still warm. Makes about 2 dozen.

Create a cozy reading corner. A comfy chair with a fleece throw,
a reading lamp and a small table for milk & cookies will encourage
your family to check out books and magazines that
you've placed on a nearby shelf.

Tommy's Big Cookie Cake

Jen Inacio
Hummelstown, PA

I get compliments every time I bake one of these! My son saw the big cookie "cakes" at the local mall and wanted one, so I created my own version for his fourth birthday. Make sure the butter is very soft, almost melted.

2-1/4 c. all-purpose flour
1 t. baking powder
1/2 t. salt
1 c. butter, softened

1-1/2 c. brown sugar, packed
1 t. vanilla extract
2 eggs
2 c. semi-sweet chocolate chips

In a small bowl, combine flour, baking powder and salt; set aside. In a large bowl, with an electric mixer on medium-high speed, beat butter, brown sugar and vanilla about 3 to 5 minutes, until mixture is creamy and has turned almost white. Add eggs, one at a time, beating well after each addition. Gradually beat in flour mixture. Stir in chocolate chips. Spread dough evenly onto a parchment paper-lined 14" round pizza pan. Bake at 350 degrees for 30 to 40 minutes, until edges turn golden. Let cool for 10 minutes in pan before removing. Cool completely; spread with Powdered Sugar Icing. Makes 10 to 15 servings.

Powdered Sugar Icing:

1 c. butter, softened
1 c. shortening
32-oz. pkg. powdered sugar

Optional: 2 to 4 T. baking cocoa
2 t. vanilla extract
2 to 3 T. milk

Combine all ingredients except milk in a large bowl. Beat with an electric mixer on medium speed until light and fluffy. Beat in milk to a spreadable consistency.

To stir up frosting in the reddest red and other extra bright colors, choose paste-style food coloring...just a dab goes a long way! Look for it at craft and cake decorating stores.

Sweet Raspberry-Oat Bars

Kathleen Sturm
Corona, CA

My mom used to make these every year for Christmas. Now I add these yummy bars to the cookie tins I share with my neighbors each holiday season.

1/2 c. margarine	1-1/2 c. long-cooking oats,
1 c. brown sugar, packed	uncooked
1-1/2 c. all-purpose flour	1/4 c. water
1/2 t. baking soda	2/3 c. seedless raspberry jam
1/2 t. salt	1 t. lemon juice

In a large bowl, blend together margarine and brown sugar until fluffy; set aside. Combine flour, baking soda and salt in a separate bowl. Stir flour mixture into margarine mixture. Add oats and water; mix together until crumbly. Firmly pat half of oat mixture into the bottom of a greased 13"x9" baking pan. In a small bowl, stir together jam and lemon juice; spread over oat mixture. Sprinkle remaining oat mixture over top. Bake at 350 degrees for 25 minutes. Cool completely before cutting into bars. Makes about 2-1/2 dozen.

An old-fashioned tin lunchbox is just the right size to use as a cookie decorating kit. Cookie cutters, colored sugars and sprinkles will fit inside nicely...everything will be right at your fingertips when it's cookie-baking time!

Peanut Butter Brownies

Debra Boyd
Gibsonia, PA

These are my kids' favorite treats. I always used to make them for camping and picnics. Even though my kids now are in their twenties and are on their own, from time to time they still ask me to make them a pan of these brownies!

1/2 c. creamy peanut butter	1 c. brown sugar, packed
1/4 c. butter, softened	2 eggs
1 t. vanilla extract	2/3 c. all-purpose flour

Blend together peanut butter, butter, vanilla and brown sugar. Add eggs, one at a time, beating well after each addition. Stir in flour. Spread mixture evenly in a well-greased 8"x8" baking pan. Bake at 350 degrees for 20 to 30 minutes, until center tests done with a toothpick. Do not overbake. Cool; spread with Peanut Butter Icing. Cut into bars. Makes 2 dozen.

Peanut Butter Icing:

1 c. creamy peanut butter   1/3 to 1/2 c. powdered sugar

In a bowl, blend together peanut butter and 1/3 cup powdered sugar. Add more powdered sugar if necessary to make a spreadable icing.

Serve brownie sundaes for an extra-special treat. Place brownies on individual dessert plates and top with a scoop of ice cream, a drizzle of chocolate or butterscotch syrup, a dollop of whipped topping and a maraschino cherry. Yummy!

Index

Index

Index

Have a taste for more?

We created our official Circle of Friends so we could
fill everyone in on the latest scoop at once.
Visit us online to join in the fun and discover free
recipes, exclusive giveaways and much more!

www.gooseberrypatch.com

Join
Our Circle of
Friends

Find
Gooseberry
Patch
in Your
Neighborhood

Find us on
Facebook

You Tube

Follow us on
twitter

Read Our
Blog

Call us toll-free at 1·800·854·6673

U.S. to Canadian recipe equivalents

Volume Measurements

1/4 teaspoon	1 mL
1/2 teaspoon	2 mL
1 teaspoon	5 mL
1 tablespoon = 3 teaspoons	15 mL
2 tablespoons = 1 fluid ounce	30 mL
1/4 cup	60 mL
1/3 cup	75 mL
1/2 cup = 4 fluid ounces	125 mL
1 cup = 8 fluid ounces	250 mL
2 cups = 1 pint =16 fluid ounces	500 mL
4 cups = 1 quart	1 L

Weights

1 ounce	30 g
4 ounces	120 g
8 ounces	225 g
16 ounces = 1 pound	450 g

Oven Temperatures

300° F	150° C
325° F	160° C
350° F	180° C
375° F	190° C
400° F	200° C
450° F	230° C

Baking Pan Sizes

Square		Loaf	
8x8x2 inches	2 L = 20x20x5 cm	9x5x3 inches	2 L = 23x13x7 cm
9x9x2 inches	2.5 L = 23x23x5 cm	Round	
Rectangular		8x1-1/2 inches	1.2 L = 20x4 cm
13x9x2 inches	3.5 L = 33x23x5 cm	9x1-1/2 inches	1.5 L = 23x4 cm